The Handbook
of Techniques for
Theatre Designers

SEBASTIAN.

Kate Ingram
Iain Stuart-
Robinson

The Handbook of Techniques for Theatre Designers

Colin Winslow

THE CROWOOD PRESS

First published in 2010 by
The Crowood Press Ltd
Ramsbury, Marlborough
Wiltshire SN8 2HR

www.crowood.com

British Library Cataloguing-in-Publication Data
A catalogue record for this book is available from the British Library.
 ISBN 978 1 84797 200 2

 Dedicated to the people who build and paint, the people who cut and sew, and all the many theatre technicians I have worked with, who have consistently made my work look better than my designs.

Frontispiece: Tinted elevation of set (detail), costume design and photographs of set model under construction for *Twelfth Night* at the Pitlochry Festival Theatre.

Typeset by Sharon Kemmett, Isis Design.
 Printed and bound in Singapore by Craft Print International.

CONTENTS

INTRODUCTION

Architects who have aimed at acquiring manual skill without scholarship have never been able to reach a position of authority to correspond to their pains, while those who relied only upon theories and scholarship were obviously hunting the shadow, not the substance. But those who have a thorough knowledge of both, like men armed at all points, have the sooner attained their object and carried authority with them.

Vitruvius (c.80/70 BC–c.15 BC)

Vitruvius, all those years ago, was writing about architects, but his remarks might apply equally to theatre designers, with whom, apart from the concept of permanence, they have much in common. He draws a careful distinction between theoretical and practical knowledge, and considers them of equal importance. Similarly, every theatre designer needs not only to possess the divine spark of artistic creativity, but also to acquire a wide range of practical skills in order to be truly proficient in his or her work. A truly creative ability is difficult to acquire if it is not possessed naturally. It is notoriously difficult to teach, needing to be nurtured and encouraged by thought, reason, discussion, argument, coupled with exposure to, and analysis of, the works of other creative artists of every kind. In fact, it may be argued that it cannot really be taught at all, which is why the spark is often considered 'divine'. This book, however, concentrates on those practical skills that almost anyone may acquire with some effort, but which are essential for a theatre designer in order to develop and communicate his creative ideas. Indeed, on many occasions the designer will find the technical resources he employs in his work can

actually assist in formulating his design concepts, acting as a spur to the creative imagination. Technique and creativity are frequently very closely intertwined.

WHAT IS THEATRE?

It is hardly possible to consider the practical skills a theatre designer will need to carry out his or her work, without some consideration of the nature of 'theatre' itself, to examine the role played by the designer in its creation. Theatre has existed, in some form, in every civilization from the earliest, most primitive societies to our technically sophisticated world of space travel and the World Wide Web: it has been ceremonial, religious, political, revolutionary, intellectual, artistic, didactic, orgiastic, cerebral or merely entertaining, but always live. It may have existed even before language itself in the form of primitive dance and ceremony, for although theatre employs language as one of its most significant tools, it is, in fact, a language in itself: one that is not solely dependent upon mere words, but one that also involves movement and imagery to a very great extent. In practically every kind of society it seems to have held a special power to fulfil some universal human need, and in times of war, revolution and violent national upheaval, somewhat surprisingly, theatre

OPPOSITE: *The amphitheatre at Epidaurus in Greece was constructed in the fifth century BC and seats 14,000 people. ©Corbis*

7

has generally flourished. Civic and religious authorities have recognized its power, at times attempting to suppress or at least censor it, and at other times encouraging it and attempting to control it as a medium for propaganda.

Throughout the ages it has demonstrated an indomitable will to survive. Indeed, it is a largely unrecognized fact that, even today, in most civilized countries, many more people attend live theatrical performances each week than football matches, and during the 2009 recession, theatre attendances in the UK showed a generally upward trend. Not only has theatre managed to survive, but, in spite of the threat from the cinema, television, and digital media of all kinds, at its best it still retains its ancient power to enthral. So what does this extraordinary phenomenon consist of? In its simplest form, theatre consists of a performer or performers communicating with an audience, even if that audience consists of only one member.

A mother telling a bedtime story to her child is a very simple, but often remarkably effective, form of theatre. On the other hand, some of the most celebrated examples of theatre have employed large numbers of actors, dancers and musicians performing before audiences of thousands. The huge amphitheatres of ancient Greece were large enough to hold virtually the entire population of a city; on the south bank of the Thames in Elizabethan London, an audience of nearly 4,000 could be crammed into the Globe Theatre; and the great Victorian actor/managers, such as Sir Henry Irving (1838–1905) and Charles Kean (1811–68) frequently employed literally hundreds of performers in their lavish revivals of Shakespeare before large and enthusiastic audiences. These, of

A modern reconstruction of Shakespeare's Globe Theatre on the South Bank of the Thames in London. PHOTO: © NIK WHEELER/CORBIS

course, are all examples of theatre taking place in elaborate purpose-built venues, constructed and designed for a particular kind of performance, but successful theatre may be created literally anywhere: a village hall, a town square, a garden, a church, a school gym or just an ordinary living-room. The theatrical communication between actor and audience is reciprocal, for the audience reacts to the performance and communicates its reaction to the performers; often by means of applause or laughter, but also through more subtle, less obvious means, which affect the performance and change it to some degree at each repetition. This, of course, is the very essence of theatre. It is something that can never occur in the cinema or on television, and it is this interaction that makes theatre unique as an art form.

The entry of Bolingbroke into London in Charles Kean's production of Richard II *at the Princess's Theatre in Oxford Street, London.*
FROM *THE ILLUSTRATED TIMES* OF 1857.

THE DESIGNER'S CONTRIBUTION

It will be seen from the above that theatrical performances can take place without any contribution from a designer whatsoever. So what role can designers play in the creation of effective theatre? They may sometimes assist by creating a sense of geographical location, a sense of period, or a specific mood or atmosphere. Their work may be realistic, stylized, or totally abstract. They can make you gasp at the wonder of their remarkable

9

creations, or they can be so discreet that you hardly notice their work at all, but if they are successful, they will have employed their artistic abilities to assist the performer in his task of communicating with the audience, whether that may be in the field of lofty intellectual concepts, low comedy, deep emotion, dazzling physical skills or simply as entertainment. This means that the stage designer's work may not always involve representational scenery or costumes in the popularly accepted sense, but, more importantly, consists of creating a special space, costumes, lighting and props that combine to place the performer into what is considered to be the best possible relationship with the audience for a specific production, whether that production is *King Lear* at the Royal National Theatre or a pop concert in the local village hall, although the end results (one hopes) will appear remarkably different, and the methods employed will vary considerably, depending upon the nature of the particular production. Historically, costume designers must have existed long before set designers. Ancient Greek vase paintings show the use of elaborate costumes and masks designed for specific theatrical performances, but someone must have decided what costumes were to be worn in primitive dance-ceremonies long before then.

The first set designers appeared centuries later to provide some kind of background to the stage action, or sometimes to create machinery for magical effects. There was no expectation of illusionistic or representational scenery in the theatres of ancient Greece, and no set designers were needed in the Elizabethan playhouses, for the stages themselves – with their balconies, doors and pillars – provided everything needed to stage most plays. No lighting designer was needed in the open-air playhouses, of course, for artificial lighting was needed only when the performances took place indoors, in the great halls of palaces and stately homes. Initially, this was provided by means of candles, later by gas, and eventually by electricity, when, for many years, stage lights were rigged and operated by in-house electricians instead of being designed by a specialist. In fact, it was not thought necessary to credit a lighting designer in

programmes until the early 1950s. Nowadays, most productions usually involve the work of several designers. Only very rarely does the same person design setting, costumes and lighting, and in the modern theatre we often also require the services of designers in other more specialized fields such as sound, video, make-up and special effects. It is therefore essential that designers have the necessary skills to communicate their concepts to a wide variety of people: not only to the technicians, such as carpenters, metal workers, painters, property makers and costumiers who will be executing the designer's work, but also to the producers, directors, performers, other designers and publicity departments, all of whom need to know what the designer has in mind. It is not necessary for the designer to have the ability to build or paint scenery, cut a pair of eighteenth-century breeches, or operate a lighting-board: these are jobs for those with more specialized skills, but if the designer cannot express his ideas in a mutually acceptable format, his creative efforts will be lost. The techniques he needs, therefore, are those of communication in various forms. Verbal communication is not enough: he must be able to convey his concepts accurately and in detail. The skills he needs to do this are wide-ranging: they encompass drawing, painting, drafting, model-making, together with an assortment of digital techniques. This book describes these skills, and offers some practical suggestions on how to acquire and develop them.

SETTING UP A STUDIO

The range of skills outlined above requires a considerable amount of equipment and materials that will not easily fit into a corner of the living room; therefore a dedicated work-room should be considered to be more or less essential, preferably one large enough to contain several distinct work areas. Drawing, painting and model-making are all activities that require table-space, so it is convenient to have more than one work surface, so that these activities can progress simultaneously. For hand-drafting, a drawing-board is essential, and, if possible, this should be big enough to accommodate an A0 size sheet of paper. (Most of your drawings will probably fit onto an A1 size sheet, but you will need some extra space around the sheet you are working on for drafting arms, etc.) Drawing-boards and other equipment for hand-drafting are discussed in more detail in Chapter 3. To use your drawing-board effectively, you will need a drafting stool. Your stool needs to be adjustable in height, and as you will probably be spending many hours at your drawing-board, it is also a good idea to invest in one with an adjustable back-support to help prevent back strain. Nowadays, many designers use computers with CAD software instead of drafting by hand, but you will find that hand-drafting is still a useful skill to acquire, particularly if you are a beginner. However, if you really intend to draft mainly from your computer, you might like to consider buying a well-designed portable drafting board that can be set up on a table top in preference to a large dedicated piece of furniture. Computer-drafting techniques are discussed in Chapter 8.

Computers need sufficient workspace around them to contain all those necessary peripherals such as mouse pad, printer, scanner, graphic pad, disk storage, etc., so don't underestimate the amount of space you will need here. You will find more detailed notes on selecting and setting up a computer installation in Chapter 8. You will inevitably be spending a great many hours seated at your computer, so make sure you have a well-

Drafting table.

Drafting stool.

Portable or desk-top drafting board.

designed chair to avoid possible back problems and RSI (repetitive strain injury). Don't underestimate the value of padded armrests to prevent painful elbows after long stretches of work at your keyboard, but bear in mind that a well-designed computer chair is one that offers the best possible ergonomic support, and is not necessarily the most relaxing one.

Very important, and frequently over-looked, is the large amount of storage space needed in a designer's studio, particularly in the form of shelving for reference books, files and models. Set models are difficult to store, simply because they are generally much too large to fit conveniently onto the average bookshelf. You might like to consider installing an extra deep shelf, at, say, just above head height, to accommodate any models you wish to keep. Painting and drawing equipment should be stored where they are easily accessible when needed. The small plastic drawer-tower units on wheels, sold by stationery suppliers such as Rymans, make excellent movable storage units for frequently needed small items. Other items tricky to store are sheets of technical drawings and the large sheets of card or mount-board needed for model-making, which will curl if not stored flat. A chart press, with wide, shallow drawers offers ideal storage for large flat sheets, but is an inconveniently large unit to fit into a studio if space is limited. Plans may be rolled and stored either standing in a bin, or in improvised canvas loops attached to the ceiling (see illustration). Storage space for large sheets of card can be improvised by attaching a piece of ply or hardboard to a convenient wall with tapes as shown in the illustration opposite.

Lighting needs particularly careful consideration: some form of halogen lights on a ceiling track, supplemented with adjustable desk lamps where needed, will provide a satisfactory and adaptable system, and an adjustable desk lamp containing a large magnifying glass can be useful for really close work. Natural light is always desirable, and artists have traditionally considered

Computer chair.

Drawer-tower storage unit.

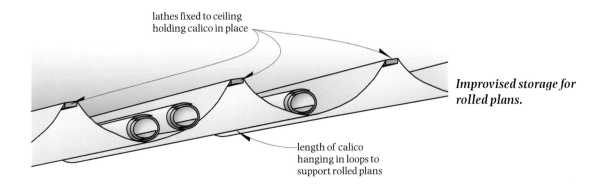

lathes fixed to ceiling
holding calico in place

*Improvised storage for
rolled plans.*

length of calico
hanging in loops to
support rolled plans

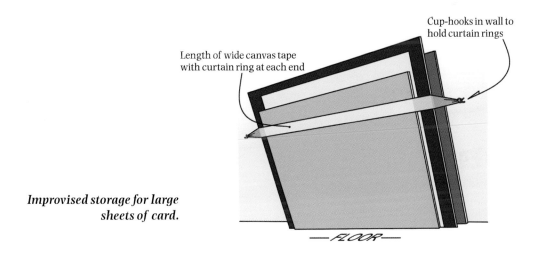

Cup-hooks in wall to
hold curtain rings

Length of wide canvas tape
with curtain ring at each end

*Improvised storage for large
sheets of card.*

— FLOOR —

northern light to be the best for studio lighting. Few of us are fortunate enough to have any choice in the direction our studio windows should face; however, very bright sunlight streaming in through a window can be a great inconvenience, causing glare across the work-surface and making computer monitor screens virtually impossible to read. Translucent window blinds, preferably white, to filter sunlight can often become a necessity. Do not hang venetian or slatted blinds, as these merely create distracting streaks of bright sunlight instead of cutting down glare. White or off-white paint is best for studio walls and ceiling to provide as much reflected light as possible. Do not use large areas of strong colour, as these will tend to tint the reflected light and distort colour perception. A large pin-board or cork wall above the work surface, on which to pin up technical drawings and other material for easy reference as you work, is more or less essential. On the floor, vinyl provides a tough, easily cleaned surface over which desk chairs on castors can run smoothly.

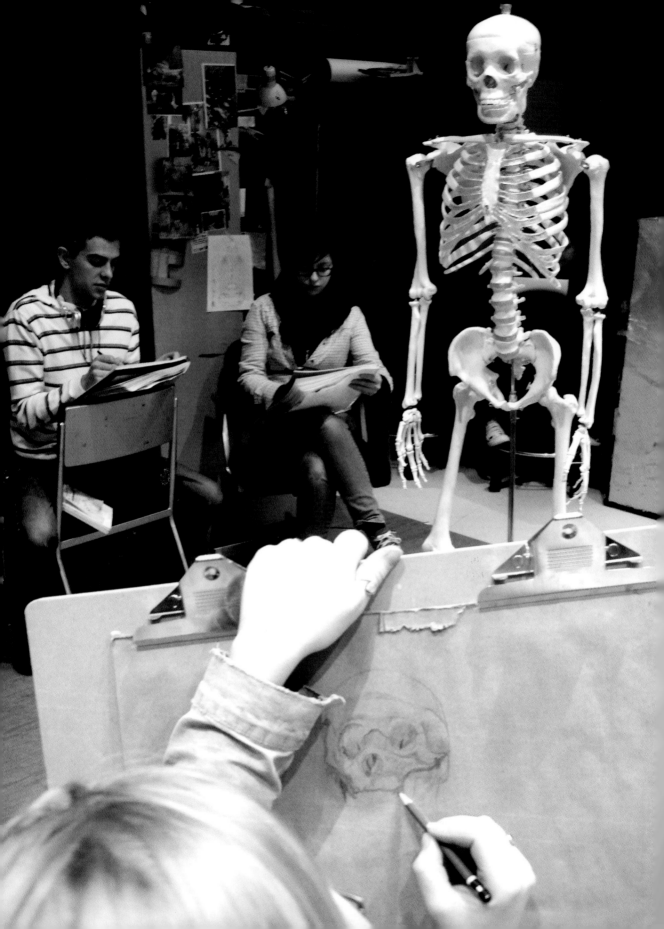

1 DRAWING AND SKETCHING

Drawing is the true test of art.

J.A.D. Ingres (1780–1867)

Almost all of the techniques a theatre designer requires involve free-hand drawing at some stage. Unfortunately, this is a skill about which many designers have a sense of insecurity. Hardly any of us will happily make the claim 'I can draw' without some qualification. However, it is not generally realized that almost anyone has the ability to develop a drawing skill to some degree, in the same way that anyone can learn the technique of playing the piano. We are frequently sent, willingly or not, to piano lessons at an early age, though there is little hope that they will turn us into concert pianists. However, we are hardly ever enrolled in drawing classes, for this is thought to be a rather esoteric skill that real artists possess naturally, and there is little hope for those of us who don't. However, attending drawing classes will help anyone to acquire a reasonably adequate drawing skill, even if there is no guarantee that it will turn us into a Michelangelo. Unfortunately, merely attending classes is not sufficient: just as the pianist needs to practise daily to improve his technique, you will need to put a similar amount of effort into developing your drawing skill. Even those lucky possessors of a good natural ability should put in the same amount of effort and turn a good skill into an excellent one.

DEVELOPING YOUR DRAWING SKILLS

Start by keeping a sketchbook, and drawing in it regularly. Buy a smallish, spiral-bound book that you can carry with you at all times, and try to draw

OPPOSITE:
Theatre design students at the University of Alberta draw from a skeleton.

RIGHT: *Typical pages from a small sketchbook.*

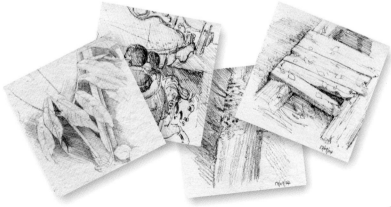

something in it every day: perhaps a rapid sketch of fellow travellers on a bus or train; or the objects on the table in front of you at a bar or café; draw your feet in the bath; draw your cat, your dog or your baby. Almost anything can become a subject for your sketchbook. The drawings do not need to be elaborate or highly developed; keep them reasonably simple and the daily sketch need never become a chore. The sketches in the illustration on page 15 were made during a walk in the woods and at a busy fun fair, and the drawing styles reflect the contrasting nature of these experiences.

Avoid caricature or slick, comic-book style drawings. The sketchbook is best used as a medium for observation, and is intended to train the eye as much as the hand. Avoid the urge to tear out pages that you feel are unsuccessful. You can learn a lot from your failed efforts. Always date your drawings in the corner of each page, and never, never throw away your old sketchbooks. When daily use of a sketchbook becomes a habit, your drawing cannot fail to improve, and your old sketchbooks will hold a graphic record of your progress. They can also bring back old friends or happy occasions more vividly than a photograph album, for your sketchbook will contain a record of small events and objects, which at the time you would not think worthy of a photograph, but which years later can acquire an unexpected significance.

LIFE CLASSES

For centuries, artists have honed their skills by drawing the human figure, clothed or naked, and today it is still considered one of the best ways for any serious artist to improve his or her technique.

If it is at all possible for you to enrol in a regular life class, you should certainly do so. You can, of course, attempt to persuade husbands, wives, partners or lovers to pose for you, but although initially they may be willing to co-operate, once they discover that you are probably never going to produce a beautiful, flattering portrait drawing worthy of framing, and that the whole procedure is really extremely uncomfortable and tedious, they

will very quickly opt out. The constant, but perfectly understandable cry of 'How much longer do I have to sit like this?' is distracting and very dispiriting. Attendance at a life class, on the other hand, has many advantages, not least that you will be setting aside a regular period in which to concentrate on nothing but drawing. You will also benefit from good advice and constructive criticism from your instructor, the opportunity to compare and discuss your work with that of fellow students, and a professional model who will never (well, hardly ever) complain. Take the trouble to learn a little about surface anatomy. It is much easier to draw something when you appreciate and understand the underlying structure. Doctors, for example, making no claim to possessing a drawing ability, can often produce remarkably good renderings of parts of the human body, merely by outlining the bone structure, then dressing it with the musculature that, to them, is very familiar. There are many helpful and comparatively inexpensive anatomy books for artists now available; some of the best contain reprints of anatomical drawings by the Old Masters such as Versalius, Michelangelo and Leonardo da Vinci. Strongly recommended are *Anatomy Lessons from the Great Masters* by Robert Beverly Hale and *Complete Anatomy and Figure Drawing* by John Raynes (*see* Bibliography).

It is helpful to spend some time drawing the human skeleton from different angles, either from the illustrations in anatomy books, or, much better, from an actual skeleton. It is, after all, the underlying framework supporting the bodies that will carry almost every costume we design. Perhaps you attend a school or college that has one available. It will well repay the effort, and your model will never complain about having to sit still.

Drawing anything is a learning experience on several levels, so by drawing the human body you are improving your knowledge of anatomy at the same time as you practise your drawing skills, and this will have a direct effect upon not only the way you render your costume designs, but your drawing technique as a whole.

A typical subject for a still-life exercise.

TOOLS FOR DRAWING

The pencil is the most popular and versatile drawing instrument available. It also happens to be the cheapest, and, perhaps for this reason, the one most often taken for granted. However, this wonderful instrument has been around for a comparatively short time in the long history of art. Graphite was discovered in Cumberland in 1504, but its potential for drawing remained unexploited until the second half of the seventeenth century, when the first graphite pencils were produced. Before that time artists had to draw in ink using a pen or a brush, or make do with the delicate but heavily indented lines that could be produced with a stylus made of silver or some other suitable metal, or with the coarse lines made by burnt wood in the form of charcoal. Great artists such as Leonardo da Vinci (1452–1519), Albrecht Dürer (1471–1528), or Michelangelo Buonarotti (1475–1564) were never able to enjoy the advantages of drawing with a graphite pencil.

Modem artists are fortunate to have such a huge, and comparatively inexpensive, range of drawing instruments available to select from, and you should experiment with as many as possible, to discover which are best suited to your individual drawing style. Try using children's crayons, soluble watercolour pencils such as those made by Caran d'Ache, or ball-point and felt-tipped pens. Look out for pens with water-soluble ink, rather than the permanent kind, for these can be worked over with water from a brush, or even simply with a moistened finger, to smudge the ink and produce effects similar to a pen-and-wash technique.

To maintain a sharp point on your pencils, you will need to have something at hand to sharpen them with. Some artists find a knife more versatile than a pencil sharpener, and the designer's studio will almost always contain a craft knife of some kind. However, do not be tempted to use the same blade you use to cut card for model-making, as using it to sharpen pencils will rapidly make the edge too blunt for really accurate cutting, and will transfer messy graphite dust to the card. If you wish to use a knife to sharpen pencils, keep a knife especially for it.

Most designers, however, prefer to use a pencil sharpener, and you may find you need two or three

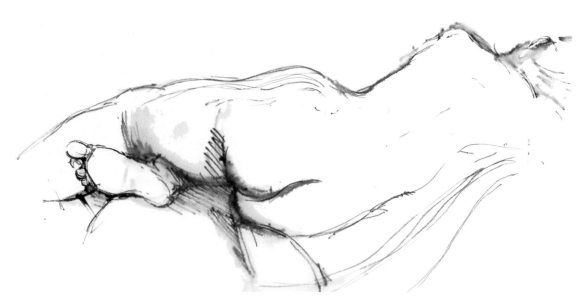

Sketch made with water-soluble pen brushed over with water.

What's Inside a Pencil and How Does It Get There?

The lead inside your pencil is not really lead, but graphite. Contrary to popular opinion, if you suck it you won't poison yourself, you will merely get a dirty tongue. Graphite was first discovered on a mountainside in Borrowdale in the north of England in 1504, and, although the local shepherds found it useful for marking sheep, it was some time before its potential as an artist's medium was realized. It became known as 'black lead' or 'plumbago' and, once its properties were recognized, it became a valuable commodity for export, as very few sources of graphite were known to exist elsewhere, and none was nearly so good as the one in Cumberland. In 1795 the supply of graphite to French artists was severely curtailed as a result of the war with England, so the French scientist, artist and pencil-maker Nicolas-Jacques Conté began to experiment with ways of improving the very inferior local supply of graphite. He found that if he ground it to a fine powder, mixed it with water, clay and wax, and baked it in a kiln, he was able to produce extremely effective pencils, with the added advantage that the degree of hardness, and the resulting blackness of the marks produced, could be regulated by the amount of clay added to the mix. These, of course, are the pencils that are still used for drawing and sketching today, and all our pencils are now graded with 'H' or 'B' numbers indicating the degree of 'hardness' or 'blackness'. Once it was realized that graphite was a valuable medium for writing and drawing, it became desirable to produce it in a more convenient form. Carpenters cut narrow grooves into a narrow plank of cedar wood and glued thin strips of graphite into them. A second, thinner plank was glued over the top, and the wood was then trimmed into pencils, and finished to the now familiar octagonal or rounded shape, creating a lucrative cottage industry around Borrowdale. Nowadays, of course, pencils are mass-produced, with a thin cylinder of lead fitted into a round groove instead of square, several pencils being cut from a single plank of wood. However, red cedar has always been considered the finest wood available for the manufacture of pencils, and is still used today.

A square groove cut into a thin strip of wood

A thin slab of graphite, sawn off a lump, inserted into the groove.

The graphite snapped off level with the top of the groove, and a thin slat of wood glued to the top, encasing the graphite.

Various pencils and the marks they make. Left to right: 2H, HB, 2B and 4B drawing pencils; black Conté pencil; sepia drawing pencil.

More drawing instruments and the marks they make. Left to right: carpenter's pencil; woodless graphite pencil; clutch lead holder with 5.6mm diameter graphite; charcoal stick; drafting pen with water-soluble ink; Caran d'Ache watercolour pencil.

An assortment of pencil sharpeners. Left to right: two-holed sharpener for thick and thin pencils; sharpener with container to catch shavings; sharpener for producing a chisel-point on carpenters' pencils; lead pointer for clutch pencils.

of them. Most convenient is, perhaps, the type that catches the shavings and graphite dust in an integrated container, but many sketching pencils are thicker than the standard drawing pencil, and some sharpeners have an especially large hole in addition to the standard one to cope with these. There is even a special sharpener designed to give a chisel-shaped point to carpenters' pencils, though you will probably never find a carpenter using one.

A block of fine sandpaper is useful to maintain a really sharp point, but can prove very messy, scattering powdered graphite over your work. If you use a 'clutch' type of pencil, a lead pointer such as the one illustrated will maintain a really sharp point without spreading graphite powder.

You will probably find that you need to use an eraser from time to time. However, force yourself to use it sparingly: most errors that need to be corrected usually occur in the early stages of a drawing, but if you start by laying out your sketch with light-weight lines they can be corrected by simply 're-stating' or drawing over them with a heavier line. Far from detracting from a drawing, these pentimenti can bring an attractive spontaneity to your sketches and help to prevent the sometimes sterile appearance of over-precise work.

Vinyl erasers work best on pencil, and it is worth buying good quality ones from a reliable manufacturer. Keep your eraser clean, and avoid rubber, which has a tendency to pick up finely powdered graphite and rub it into the surface of the paper, creating black smudges which then become impossible to remove. The little bit of rubber that is sometimes attached to the end of a pencil is generally useless and should be ignored.

DRAWING PAPER

Art stores usually stock a wide and somewhat confusing range of papers, which varies considerably in quality and price. There's little doubt that the highly priced handmade papers provide by far the best surface for drawing, but the very fine quality and high cost can be intimidating, and are often the cause of overly tentative drawings lacking the rather attractive, careless spontaneity of those done on cheaper grades of paper. For this reason, it is a good idea to keep a stock of cheap grades for sketches and roughs, and buy higher grades as and when they are needed for final designs, striving to retain some of the spontaneity of the earlier sketches. Whichever paper you choose, before you buy, check the 'tooth' quality; this simply means the degree of roughness to the surface. Some papers are finished to a very smooth, slightly waxy surface, which is ideal for graphic design work but unsympathetic to many of the drawing media commonly used for sketching. Gently run a finger over the paper, and look for those that have a slightly roughened, 'floury' feel to the surface. The cheapest paper available is probably newsprint. This is a recycled paper of the kind used for printing newspapers, generally with a 'natural' off-white colour, rather than the bleached white of higher grades. Its main disadvantages are a tendency to tear very easily, and its high degree of absorbency, which makes it generally unsuitable to use for wash techniques. It is sold in large sheets, or, more economically, by the roll, which you can slice into sheets of a convenient size and staple onto a cardboard backing to make a handy rough sketchbook. Cartridge paper is a better quality, heavy weight paper originally used in the manufacture of cartridge cases for weaponry. It is a good standard quality paper for drawing and painting, usually with a fine 'toothed' surface which is ideal for most jobs. It can be bought in large sheets or bound into sketchbooks. The best art papers are made by hand, although most 'handmade' papers are now, somewhat illogically, produced by machinery. They are made from wood or rag fibres mixed with water, distributed over a fine mesh sieve, and drained. The resulting mat of tangled fibres is then pressed to remove all the remaining water, and allowed to dry. The mesh produces a noticeably different texture to the surface than the more natural texture of the other side. Genuine handmade papers characteristically taper to a thin, uneven edge produced by the side of the sieve-screen, and always contain the manufacturer's watermark. Hold the paper up to the light and check: when the watermark reads the right way round, then you are looking at the side of the paper you are intended to work on, but do not feel inhibited by this if you prefer to work on the 'wrong' side. The finished papers may be pressed by the manufacturer to remove some or all of the naturally textured surface, and are generally available in three grades of roughness: the smoothest grade is referred to as 'hot-pressed' or 'HP'. Next in roughness comes 'not-hot-pressed'

(often called just 'not'), or 'cold-pressed' (CP). The roughest grade, logically enough, is referred to as 'rough'. Hot-pressed paper is probably most suitable for fine detailed work in pencil or pen, but for work with charcoal, Conté or wash, not-pressed is the popular choice. Rough grade paper is best confined to loose, heavily textured watercolour techniques.

You will probably find that your art store also stocks a large number of specialist papers in a wide variety of colours and textures, and it is worth experimenting with these. Tinted Ingres papers with a distinct 'tooth' are available in a wide range of textures and colours, which will allow the creative use of white for adding highlights. The subtle greys or beiges are generally preferable to the very intense colours, which are too dominant to serve as a background. Ingres papers are often sold in convenient spiral-bound sketchbooks containing a range of several different papers. It can be very rewarding to make your own paper, and many books are available that will take you step-by-step through the techniques involved. The sketchbook pages reproduced on page 15 are all drawn on a very rough, naturally-tinted home-made paper produced from recycled waste. An extraordinarily wide range of plants and other organic materials can be incorporated into home-made papers to produce interesting textures; however, you should be prepared for a very messy experience.

Paper always expands when wet, and shrinks as it dries. This can cause serious problems when using very watery techniques such as pen-and-wash or watercolour, for as the water is usually applied to only a small part of the paper at a time, the wet areas will first expand, then shrink to form a buckled, uneven surface. You can avoid this by pre-stretching the paper over a drawing-board. The technique works best with better quality handmade papers, but you can also use it with cartridge paper. First wet the paper in a large sink or bath, then gently smooth it over a strong drawing-board, at least 2cm (1in) wider than the paper all round. Smooth by pressing with a clean cloth: do not rub, as it is easy to damage the surface when the paper is wet. Then fix it to the board along all edges, using brown gummed paper strip (the kind that needs to be moistened to stick) about 5cm (2in) wide. Note that sticky tapes such as drafting tape, mounting tape, Sellotape or Scotch tape will not work for this, as the gum must be able to stick to a wet surface. First tape down one of the longer sides, then the side opposite to the first, and finally the two shorter sides. Gluing them down in this order will help to prevent wrinkles appearing as it dries. Other sheets can be added straight on top of the first, each sheet being taped individually to the board. When all layers (about six or eight) have been stuck down, push a drawing pin (or thumb tack) into each corner of the board, through all the layers of gummed tape, and leave to dry flat. As it dries, the paper will shrink and tighten to drum-skin smoothness. As each sheet is used, it can be removed by slicing through the gummed paper strip with a knife to uncover the layer beneath. It is important to use a really sturdy board as a base, as it has to withstand considerable pressure as the paper contracts, and a thin board will warp or even break. This technique produces an excellent surface for final costume designs or set renderings, but you will probably not want to go to these lengths for rough work. The rather tedious and messy task of stretching wet paper over a board can be simplified and speeded up if necessary by using a comparatively small board, or even a piece of hardboard (or masonite): fold the edges of the wet paper over each side of the board in turn, and hold them in place with 'Bulldog'-type binder clips until the paper is thoroughly dry. The clips may be removed when the paper is completely dry, as it will then have shrunk around the board sufficiently to hold itself in place. Pads of pre-prepared watercolour paper can be bought from art-stores, but they are never quite as good as those you prepare for yourself.

DRAWING STYLES

Ideally, the designer needs to develop not one, but several drawing styles, each fitted to a different purpose. We readily admit that the technical drawing skills required to produce stage plans and working drawings are in a different category from the drawing skills needed to produce, say, a costume design; but we also need to develop a very rapid, much less refined drawing skill to sketch out ideas when in discussion with a director or technicians, and also some knowledge of basic perspective techniques to produce a convincing rendering of a stage set when this is required.

The rapid sketching technique is inevitably the drawing style a designer needs to use most frequently. It is hardly possible to have any kind of discussion about the work in hand without reaching for a drawing instrument. Even the directors we work with will sometimes reach for a pen or pencil, though, feeling a little inhibited by the tool in their hand and the presence of a designer, they will probably preface any marks they make with 'I can't draw, of course, but....' Confident quick sketches made by the designer often turn out to have an attractive vitality that later, more carefully considered work sometimes lacks, so do not discard these initial sketches. It's a good idea to keep all the paperwork connected with a particular job in one folder, including any letters or emails, your contract, telephone numbers and addresses of contacts, and, of course, all your roughs, even those done hastily on paper napkins or the backs of beer-mats. They can be invaluable for reference or inspiration when creativity flags, and sometimes provide a practical basis for a final design. In addition to a 'quick and dirty' rough sketch style, the designer also needs to develop a clearer and more precise free-hand style to communicate comparatively elaborate concepts in detail. This is the style used for describing the finer details of costume designs, for example, when technical drawings of the kind produced when designing scenery are obviously inappropriate.

Somewhere between the 'quick and dirty' sketch and the carefully rendered costume detail, is the style the designer will use to produce most finished costume designs. Ideally, this style should retain some of the attractive immediacy of the

Rough concept sketches.

rough sketch, but also contain a sufficient degree of accuracy to fulfil its primary purpose of clearly conveying the designer's intentions. Costume designs are discussed in greater depth in Chapter 7.

PRACTICAL EXERCISES

1. **Rendering textures.** Make a rapid freehand pencil sketch of a cube in perspective. Make the cube roughly 6cm (2½in) high. Decide which direction the light is coming from, and add a little tone to give the cube a three dimensional appearance. You can add a cast shadow if you wish. Now draw a whole series of cubes of a

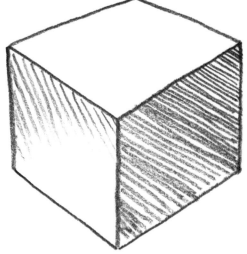

Pencil sketch of a simple cube.

Detail drawing of a period doublet.

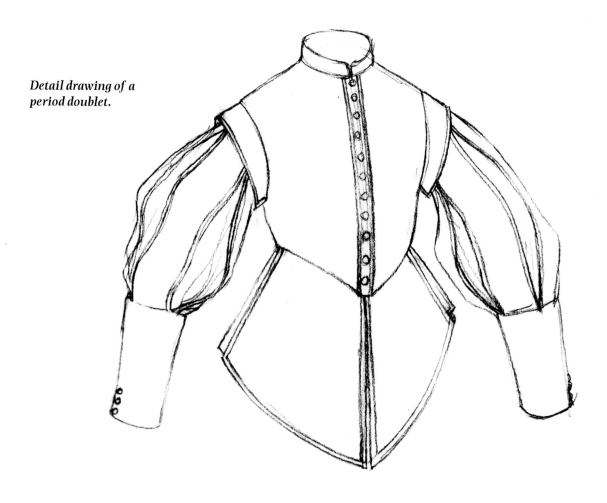

similar size, using only your pencil to suggest that each cube is made of a different material such as wood, stone, marble, steel, glass, fur, jelly or anything else you can imagine. Each rendering should clearly show both the material the cube is made of, and the direction of the light hitting it.

2. **Reproducing textures.** Take a walk in a park or some woods (take your sketchbook with you, of course) and bring back some very small pieces of organic material such as a tiny piece of bark, a stone chip, a sliver of fungus or a fragment of lichen. Whatever it is, it should be very tiny, around 5mm (¼in) across. When you get home, lay the objects out on a sheet of white paper and examine them very carefully. Use a magnifying glass if you wish. Select one of your samples that has an interesting texture, and using the largest sheet of paper you can find (at least A1 or ANSI D), attach the subject near to one side of the paper where you can easily observe it, and draw it as large as you possibly can, taking up most of the sheet of paper, and using whatever drawing instrument you feel is most appropriate. Draw as large as possible, taking up most of the sheet of paper. Examine your subject very carefully, and reproduce the texture as accurately as you possibly can. The result can often be a surprisingly interesting and attractive drawing, with a semi-abstract

quality. As the exercise will probably take you some time to complete, do not attempt to finish it all in one go. Try working on it for a short period each day, and critically assess the previous day's work at the start of each new drawing session.

3. **Rendering glass.** Find a bottle or jar made of tinted glass or plastic and place it on its side, turned at an angle to your line of vision to produce about a three-quarter view. First sketch in the major shapes (the outline of the bottle, for example), then secondary shapes, including all the many reflection shapes you can see in the glass. Suggest the label, rendering any letters as shapes or texture rather than meaningful words. Work primarily in line, using a B or 2B pencil with a very sharp point. You may add some shading to indicate lights and darks, but restrict yourself to no more than two or three distinct levels of tone. Note that 'shininess' is best suggested by strong, sharp contrasts between dark and light tones. Draw at life-size or larger.

4. **A still life.** Set up a small group of objects of contrasting shapes and textures. Do not make the group too large or elaborate: three or four objects are usually sufficient. If possible, include something shiny and hard, something organic, and something made of fabric. Position the group, or adjust the lighting to obtain the maximum effect of contrasting light and shade, including cast shadows. Lay out the entire group on your page with a sharp B or 2B pencil, lightly sketching in all the objects to establish the general position of the still-life on the page, then work over the group, correcting and reinforcing all the shapes, and paying particular attention to 'negative shapes' (i.e. the shapes of the spaces between objects). Gradually build up texture and form with layers of shading and cross-hatching, but do not attempt a photographic reality. Try to restrict yourself to only two or three distinct layers of rapidly applied tone, and let the medium you are using speak for itself. The result should look like an attractive pencil-drawing, not a photograph.

2   USING COLOUR

Colour is notoriously difficult to quantify. Describing a wall in my house, I might tell you that it is 5m wide by 3m high (or 16ft by 10ft) and you would have an accurate impression of its dimensions, but when I try to describe the colour, it is impossible to be so precise: I might say that it is 'a kind of yellowish-cream', or I could mention that the paint I used was called 'Harvest Gold', but you would still have only the vaguest idea of the colour I am describing. In an effort to be more precise, I could mention that the colour is Pantone 13-0850 TPX, described by Pantone as 'Aspen Gold', but this would mean nothing unless you had the (rather expensive) Pantone colour-swatch book at hand to look up the number.

However, even if you had the Pantone swatches to refer to, the colour on my wall would probably appear quite different in my house, lit by late

OPPOSITE: *Working on costume designs such as these for* The Snow Queen *at the Theatre Royal, York, encourages the designer towards an extravagant use of colour.*

The Pantone Colour System

Pantone was originally a comparatively insignificant company that made colour cards for the cosmetics industry, but in 1962 it was bought by an employee, Lawrence Herbert, who immediately set out to develop a colour-matching system that could be universally applied regardless of the method used to produce the colours. He created swatch books containing a large number of colours organized in a convenient fan format, which could be identified, not only by name, but also by a precise numerical system. The Pantone Guides are normally printed on small sheets of thin card measuring 15cm × 5cm (6in × 2in), each page containing a series of related colours identified numerically. The PANTONE® MATCHING SYSTEM® has been used as a standard reference by graphic designers and printing houses all over the world for many years, and has now expanded its system to include digital technology and many other industries where precise colour matching is essential. However much care is taken, colours will always change slightly over time, and are affected by climate, the nature of the inks, and the paper they are printed on. For this reason, Pantone recommends that for really accurate colour matching, the swatch books should be replaced yearly. Fortunately stage designers rarely need to work with such extreme precision.   Lawrence Herbert retired from his position of CEO, Chairman, and President of the company in 2007.

afternoon sunlight, than it does on your small colour swatch, viewed beneath a tungsten desk-lamp. The physical size of the area of colour also plays a part: how many times have we carefully selected a colour from the postage-stamp sized swatches supplied by paint manufacturers and been surprised by the result when a whole room has been painted in that colour? There is a scale in colour just as in dimension, and for this reason, experienced scene painters will sometimes mix the colours they use to paint scenery just a little paler than the colour the designer has used to paint the set model to compensate for this, and represent the designer's intentions rather than the precise colour. We have, of course, no real way of establishing that the colour you see on my painted wall is exactly the same colour as the one I see, even if we were both standing side by side looking at it under exactly the same lighting conditions. If you could see through my eyes, it might appear totally different, which may be a reason for personal colour preferences; always an additional complication in any discussion about colour.

COLOUR PSYCHOLOGY

There is an underlying psychology in the use of colour that the theatre designer cannot afford to ignore. The development of synthetic colours in the early twentieth century and, more recently, new cheaper and faster printing and dyeing techniques that have the ability to reproduce a wider range of colours than the eye can actually distinguish, mean that colour choices are no longer restricted by considerations of economy, or even by generally accepted standards of good taste.

However, old habits die hard, and pink is still the preferred colour for girl-babies, and blue for boy-babies. Even in these days of gender-equality, pinkish tones are still favoured for the walls of public washrooms for women (or so I am informed), and white sugar is still sold in mainly blue packaging, for marketing experts have determined that blue suggests 'sweetness', and green (never used to package sugar) suggests 'astringency'. In the 1970s, candidates being interviewed for important executive positions were frequently subjected to a Lüscher Colour Test in an attempt to find out if their personalities were compatible with the job applied for. This ostensibly very simple test is administered by asking subjects to place eight coloured cards in order of preference, and the colour sequence is then interpreted along the lines laid down in the Lüscher handbook. The subject does not usually realize that the colours rejected carry equal, or possibly more, significance as the colours preferred. Although nowadays treated with justifiable suspicion, the results, when correctly interpreted, can often be a startlingly accurate indication of personality traits.

We are probably right to treat a psychological evaluation based solely upon colour choice with scepticism, but most of us have observed that a person who persistently dresses in, say, black or dark neutral colours, has a different type of personality than one who prefers strong, vibrant colours, or one who wears pale, pastel tones. The same applies to the colours we choose to paint our homes. Public spaces such as hospitals, dentists' waiting rooms, and airport lounges tend to be painted in subdued, neutral tones in an attempt to relax their frequently apprehensive occupants, but in our living rooms we are allowed free rein to express our personalities, and this can sometimes result in colour schemes which, although we love

The cards used in the Lüscher Colour Test demonstrate a rather off-beat range of colours.

them personally, can make visitors feel distinctly ill at ease. Hence the success of television programmes that show how a simple redecoration scheme can make un-saleable homes more attractive to potential buyers. Red is a colour that universally suggests liveliness, action and passion. (Also, somewhat contradictorily, 'Stop!', which is why Chairman Mao, out of respect for the Red Flag, once suggested reversing the colours of Chinese traffic lights.) Blue, on the other hand, tends to suggest peace, relaxation and inactivity.

This kind of consideration should also affect the colours we select in all aspects of design work in the theatre. Pretty pinks hardly seem appropriate for, say, the gloomy introspection of a play by Strindberg, but a frivolous light comedy might demand the use of frivolous light colours to achieve its aim. Similarly, we must carefully analyse the personalities of the characters who will wear our costumes before committing ourselves to colour choices. Some plays change their character as the plot develops: Shakespeare's *Twelfth Night* is a case in point, switching from joyous comedy to perplexing cruelty when the jokes are carried too far, and Malvolio is locked in a darkened cell. Here the lighting designer can be particularly helpful, by sympathetically changing the atmosphere with a subtle modulation of the lighting, replacing some of the warm, attractive colours used to enhance the earlier scenes with cooler, more sombre colours. Once again, collaboration is crucial to artistic creativity.

COLOUR WHEELS

Artists and scientists have attempted to create a definitive system of colour notation since the early eighteenth century by constructing diagrams, usually in the form of a segmented disc or 'wheel'. In Britain we may have been introduced to a simplified version of the Ostwald colour system at school, whereas in America the Munsell system was more popular. Both systems posited three primary colours: red, yellow and blue arranged in the form of a wheel, with secondary colours between them, produced by combining the two primary colours at each side. More elaborate colour wheels included tertiary colours, formed by

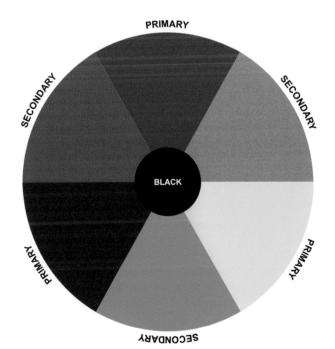

Colour wheel showing primary and secondary colours.

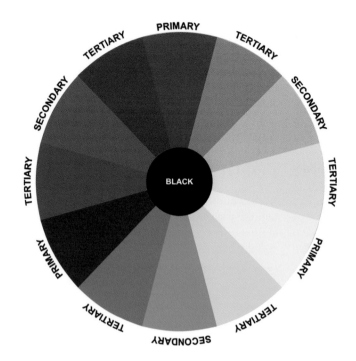

Colour wheel including tertiary colours formed by combining secondary and primary colours.

combining the secondary colours (see illustrations). However, these were by no means the only systems, and artists in other nations or societies worked from quite different principles. For example, in classical Japanese painting, the primary, or 'parent' colours in combination with black and white produce a much wider range of secondary colours (see opposite). Most of these systems have a great deal to recommend them as methods of quantifying colour relationships. Many of them go astray, however, when they attempt to use the system to quantify good taste or 'colour harmony'. The earlier systems, particularly, formulated rules for the best use of colour based upon the colour wheels: combinations of colours that lay adjacent to each other on the wheel, such as red and purple, or yellow and green, were considered 'harmonious' and therefore desirable, whereas colours opposite each other, such as blue and orange or yellow and purple, were looked upon as 'inharmonious' and unacceptable. (The writer well remembers being smacked at primary school for painting an orange pattern against a blue background in defiance of the Ostwald Colour Circle printed on the lids of our

paint boxes.) On the other hand, the classical Japanese rules of colour harmony in painting forbid the use of a 'parent' colour touching any secondary colour of which it forms a component.

Yellow, for example, may not be used next to green, or white next to sky blue. (No white clouds in a blue sky?) In a world where the totally free use of colour in fashion, graphics and interior decoration is considered the norm, these rules seem bizarre. But every decade has colour combinations that are considered fashionable or trendy, and the interior decoration 'make-over' programmes on television still propound 'rules' for ensuring a tasteful use of colour involving frequent use of terms such as 'accent colours' or 'colour-focus'. In stage design, of course, we use colours in combinations that are sometimes deliberately clashing or disquieting, or suggestive of some previous period, to obtain a desired effect. Rules are non-existent, but there are some important considerations to be borne in mind: most theatres are dark places, and, apart from those occasions when a show is to be presented in the open air and in broad daylight, a lighting designer must arrange lanterns or luminaires ('instruments' in North

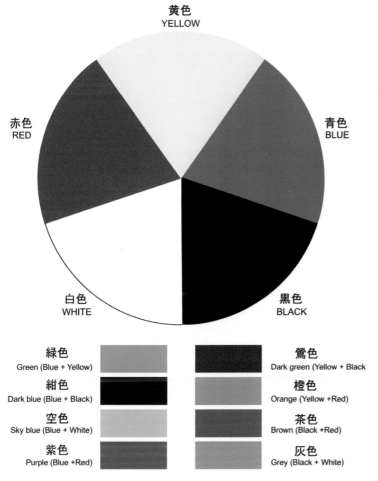

黄色
YELLOW

赤色
RED

青色
BLUE

白色
WHITE

黒色
BLACK

A Japanese colour wheel with five 'parent' colours and eight secondary colours.

綠色 Green (Blue + Yellow)		鶯色 Dark green (Yellow + Black
紺色 Dark blue (Blue + Black)		橙色 Orange (Yellow +Red)
空色 Sky blue (Blue + White)		茶色 Brown (Black +Red)
紫色 Purple (Blue +Red)		灰色 Grey (Black + White)

America) in an appropriate manner to reveal the productions to their audiences. The lights are usually coloured with tinted gels, sometimes with a high degree of intensity, which will change the colours selected by the set or costume designer to a very great extent. Designers must collaborate, therefore, to evaluate any colours to be used on stage in combination with the colour of the lights under which they are to be seen. Knowing, for example, that a happy, up-beat chorus number in a pantomime or musical show will probably be lit in warm, pinkish tones, the costume designer may decide to exclude strong greens from his palette (*see* 'Unlucky Green?' on page 38).

The colours that the paint manufacturers put into the little tubes we buy at the art store are extremely intense. For most work, they are far too intense to use straight from the tube and the colours will generally need to be modified considerably before they can be applied to a design. Colours are often classified by the terms 'hue' (indicating the actual colour), 'tint' (indicating that white has been added to make a paler version of the colour), or 'shade' (indicating that black has been added to make a darker colour). Try mixing colours with grey to reduce intensity, or white or black for subtle tints and shades; or mix them with other colours to modify the hue, and you will create a palette consisting of an infinite range of colours from just a small handful of pigments. Colours are often referred to as being 'warm' or 'cold'. Reds and oranges, for example, are very

33

warm colours, whereas blues are cold colours. Greens sit somewhere in the middle, and browns can be either warm or cool, depending on the amount of red they contain.

Analyse the colours you see around you. They are usually much more subtle than they may appear at first glance. For instance, the browns found in nature are never as intense as the browns in the colourist's tubes. Your furniture may be stained by the manufacturer to a rich dark brown, but in nature, tree-trunks and old wood are rarely a true brown. If you examine them, you will see that they are very subtle combinations of greys, greens and yellows; and stone, although frequently described as 'grey', is much more subtle in hue than the dull grey produced by simply mixing black and white together. Try adding a little brown, blue, green or yellow to greys in your design work. The pure, but monotonous grey produced from a

---

Terms Used to Describe Colours

hue – just another name for colour.

tint – any colour with white added to make it paler.

shade – any colour with black added to make it darker.

tone – the lightness or darkness of a colour as opposed to its hue.

intensity – the strength (brightness or dullness) of a colour.

primary colours – red, yellow and blue in pigment: three colours that cannot be obtained by mixing other colours.

secondary colours – colours such as green, orange and purple that can be made by mixing two primary colours together.

intermediate or tertiary colours – colours such as orangey-reds or yellowy-greens, made by mixing a primary and a secondary colour together.

complementary colours – pairs of colours that, taken together, contain all three primary colours, such as red + green; orange + blue; or blue/green + red/orange. Complementary colours are situated directly opposite each other on a conventional colour wheel.

key colour – the dominant colour in a colour scheme or mixture of colours.

---

mixture of black and white is best confined to the sides of battleships.

USING A RESTRICTED PALETTE

Examine the two designs over the page: they are front cloth designs from pantomimes at the Theatre Royal, York, each of which contained around twelve to fifteen different scenes. Apart from the fact that one represents a jungle, and the other a cellar, they are further differentiated by the use of strongly contrasted colour palettes, each of which is severely restricted by deliberately omitting one of the primary colours. The first design contains no red, but makes use of blue, yellow, black and white in many combinations. The second design contains no blue, but uses red, yellow, black and white. The designs shown here demonstrate extreme examples of the restricted palette technique used for short scenes in multi-scene shows. However, in a much modified form, it can be remarkably effective, not only for painted cloths, but for sets of almost any type or style.

The design at the top of page 36 is for part of the Act 1 set for a touring production of *On Approval* by Frederick Lonsdale. The play begins in a smart Mayfair flat in the 1920s, and the pieces illustrated show the design for a mural painted on the walls. It was important that the mural should not detract the audience's attention from the action of the play, so a severely restricted palette was used, at a very low intensity, with a sizeable quantity of pale grey added to each colour. If you feel it is appropriate, try adding some final touches of the omitted colour to a design based on a restricted palette, and you will find it 'sings' in a way that it never could against a multicoloured background. This trick is demonstrated in the painted cloth design reproduced on page 102, where the 'orphan' colour is a fairly strong rose-pink. Conversely, a design containing a range of strongly contrasted colours can sometimes be unified by adding just a very little of a key colour to each of the colours in the design. This trick can be useful to harmonize jarring colours when required, producing an effect a little like using a

Pantomime cloth design using a restricted palette, omitting red.

Pantomime cloth design using a restricted palette, omitting blue.

35

Set design using a restricted palette at very low intensity.

Colour wheel showing primary and secondary colours of light.

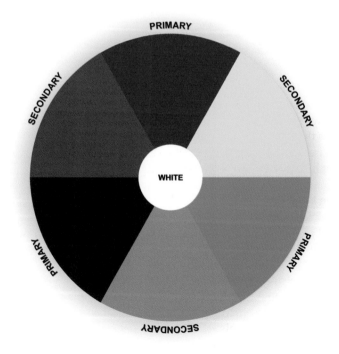

tinted light source. Do not look upon the techniques outlined above as 'rules' for the use of colour. In spite of Ostwald, Munsell *et al.* there are no rules, so you must experiment continually, and discover what techniques work best for you.

THE COLOURS OF LIGHT

The primary colours of light are not the same as the primary colours of pigment: somewhat surprisingly, they are red, blue and green. They can be mixed to produce magenta (red and blue); cyan (blue and green); and yellow (green and red). If all three primary colours are mixed together at full intensity they produce white light, although in practice, it is never 'pure' white, as the colour media we use do not produce really pure primary colours, and 100 per cent intensity is a theoretical concept rather than a practical reality. Computers handle light much more effectively, for a monitor screen reproduces images in the form of coloured light, using a similar 'additive' system of colour mixing, which often causes puzzlement to those mixing colours in programmes such as Photoshop for the first time. Note that if it were possible to obtain absolutely pure primary colours of pigment (red, yellow and blue) and mix them together in equal amounts at full intensity, they would logically produce black; and by not applying any pigment at all to a colourless surface we are left with white; whereas when mixing light, precisely the reverse happens: by not applying any light at all we are left with black (or total darkness). The fact that light and pigment work in opposite ways causes some complications when coloured light is applied to a coloured surface, – a commonplace occurrence on stage. However, these phenomena can be used to the designer's advantage, by the use of coloured light to enhance the colours in the set and costumes – or, alternatively, to modulate or subdue them when this is desirable. Generally speaking, lights tinted a warm colour such as a very pale rose can be relied upon to create a sense of well-being and to flatter skin tones, so they are often employed when lighting comedies. The pale ambers or 'straw' colours can also flatter, but tend to create a rather less glamorous effect than the pinks. Blue lighting media, especially the deep blues, greatly reduce the lights' intensity, but are really useful in creating atmosphere – especially, of course, in night scenes. Greens are generally best reserved for special effects such as the one described below, or for the appearance of the Demon King in pantomime. (Another instance of the need to consider the colour of light when designing costumes: there has rarely been a Demon King without a green spotlight, so red may not be the best colour choice for his costume.)

The theatre-going public is often surprised when it discovers that almost all the lights used on stage are coloured to some degree, to create subtle mood or atmospheric effects. However, few lighting designers would consider using the same colour in all their lights, or setting them all at the same intensity, for stage lighting is not used merely to reveal the on-stage action. It is also used to model features of performers and of the set itself, and a subtle contrast between warm colours, say, for front and side lighting, and colder colours for light coming from the back or opposite side, will usually produce sharper modelling of the actors' faces and enhance the sculptural quality of the set.

The base colour in any indoor stage is black. The audience usually sits in darkness, and black legs and borders are used to mask the sides and tops of stage sets when required. For this reason, when painting set designs, it is often helpful to deploy paint in a similar manner to the way the lighting designer uses light: light is generally concentrated on the central acting area, so it can sometimes be effective to darken the colours of the set as they approach the periphery of the stage, creating a slightly 'vignetted' appearance. An airbrush is an excellent tool to do this on the coloured designs or the set model, and the scene painters will probably use a paint-spray to reproduce the effect on the full-sized set. The photograph on page 39 of a set for *The Caretaker* illustrates the use of this technique. For this rather unnerving play, some surrounding gloom is quite appropriate, but even the bright, cloudy backdrop for Mother Goose on page 102 employs a similar technique to some extent, by darkening the colours towards the edges.

Unlucky Green?

I have never admitted that I am more than twenty-nine, or thirty at the most. Twenty-nine when there are pink shades, thirty when there are not.

Mrs Erlynne in *Lady Windermere's Fan*
by Oscar Wilde.

There is a long-standing theatrical superstition that green is an unlucky colour when used on stage, and the writer painfully remembers designing costumes for a very well-known and talented actress who steadfastly refused to wear a green dress designed for her for this very reason. However, like many superstitions, this one is actually grounded in practicality, for the most flattering light to ageing skin is probably a pale rose-pink, but this colour would tend to make a green dress or a green set look very drab, and the lighting designer might have to resort to some other colour, much less flattering to the performers. On the other hand, this effect can sometimes be used to advantage: imagine that in Act 2, Scene 1 of a production of *A Midsummer Night's Dream*, Oberon is wearing a full-length red cloak. The forest at night would logically be fairly darkly lit. If, with his line '… I am invisible, And I will overhear their conference' he wraps himself in his cloak and the lighting designer hits him with a diffused green spotlight at the same time, the green light will render the red cloak extremely dull and dark, and, against the dark set, the actor will become, almost literally, invisible.

COLOUR AND PAINT

We are taught at school that colour is observed by light of different wavelengths entering the eye through the pupil and falling on the retina at the back of the eye, which contains two kinds of light receptors referred to as 'rods' and 'cones' because of their distinctive shapes. In daylight, the eye sees by the colour-sensitive cones reacting to the specific wavelength of the light they receive to create the perception of colour, although precisely

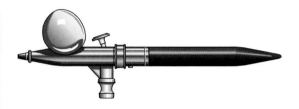

An airbrush produces an extremely fine spray that is useful for subtly toning designs and set models.

how this works is still not clearly understood. At night, or in dim light, the eye sees mainly with the rods, which are good at distinguishing light and shade, but not very sensitive to colour. The information received by the rods and cones is transmitted to the brain via the optic nerve from the back of the retina, and the brain then interprets this information as it receives it. It appears, therefore, that colour, like beauty, is quite literally 'in the eye of the beholder', and in far-off prehistoric times, before any sighted creatures roamed the earth, the phenomenon of colour must not have existed at all. Nowadays, when we wish to work with colours we buy various substances at the art store that reflect light in a particular wavelength, and apply them to a surface of an object to trick the eye into thinking the object is the colour we wish it to see. These substances, of course, constitute paint in various forms. However, it took many generations for paints to achieve the high degree of sophistication they have today. Not too long ago, artists had to mix their own paints using imported natural pigments from a wide variety of remote sources, many of which were scarce and costly. Before a natural pigment can be used, it must first be refined, mixed with a liquid medium such as water for easy application, and with an adhesive medium to make it adhere to the surface when all the water has evaporated. Until comparatively recently, scene painters were very familiar with this process, as they had to go through the tedious process of combining dry pigments with an animal glue called 'size', melted

Set for Harold Pinter's **The Caretaker** *at the Manitoba Theatre Centre in Winnipeg, Canada.*

in water and mixed to just the right consistency to make it useable. Now we are fortunate to have emulsion or latex paints ready for use in convenient cans from suppliers such as Rosco; moreover, since the discovery of aniline dyes by William Perkin in 1856, we have a huge range of inexpensive, intense synthetic colours that would have astonished the Old Masters. Designers generally prefer to use water-based paints for set models and costume renderings rather than the oil paints preferred by the Old Masters, but these come in several varieties, and it is sometimes difficult to decide between them. The type of paint you choose depends a lot upon personal preference, but you should be aware of their distinctive qualities.

Watercolour is available in tubes or in semi-moist 'pans' or 'cakes'. The colours are transparent, and are best used as tinted washes overlaying each other to create subtle combinations of hues and shades. Traditionally, the watercolour palette does not contain white, as tints are produced by allowing the white paper to show through a thin, watery wash; however, Chinese White is available to use as a 'body' colour if this is desired. Quality varies considerably, from

cheap children's paint boxes to the much more expensive 'artists' quality' colours; the higher quality ranges offer purer, more intense colours with greatly improved 'mixability'. Gouache is probably the most popular type of paint for general design purposes; in fact it is often referred to as 'designers' colour'. It has the advantage of being able to be used as an opaque medium that can cover underlying areas, or it can be thinned down to produce an effect similar to watercolour. It is available only in tubes.

Acrylic paints are latex based, and are preferred by a great many designers for their exceptional brilliance. They can be used in much the same way as gouache, but tend to dry to a somewhat 'plastic' sheen, particularly when thickly applied. They are excellent for large areas of flat colour, particularly in situations where it may need to be handled, but can also be diluted for more subtle effects. Avoid the cheap 'poster' colours often used in school art classes: they tend to look 'chalky' when dry, and easily lose their integrity when mixed together, rapidly degrading to the colour and texture of Thames mud. In addition to paints applied with brushes in a conventional manner, theatre

Designers Gouache Colour Chart

Winsor & Newton's colour chart of Designers Gouache. (Colour chart courtesy of Winsor & Newton.)

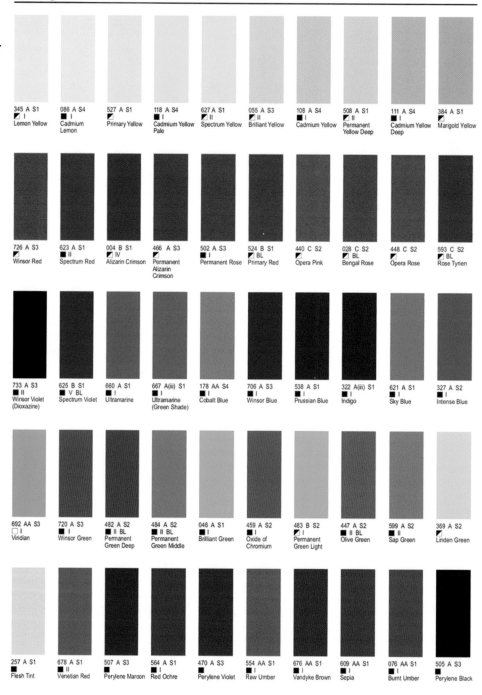

| 345 A S1 | 086 A S4 | 527 A S1 | 118 A S4 | 627 A S1 | 055 A S3 | 108 A S4 | 508 A S1 | 111 A S4 | 384 A S1 |
| Lemon Yellow | Cadmium Lemon | Primary Yellow | Cadmium Yellow Pale | Spectrum Yellow | Brilliant Yellow | Cadmium Yellow | Permanent Yellow Deep | Cadmium Yellow Deep | Marigold Yellow |

| 726 A S3 | 623 A S1 | 004 B S1 | 466 A S3 | 502 A S3 | 524 B S1 | 440 C S2 | 028 C S2 | 448 C S2 | 593 C S2 |
| Winsor Red | Spectrum Red | Alizarin Crimson | Permanent Alizarin Crimson | Permanent Rose | Primary Red | Opera Pink | Bengal Rose | Opera Rose | Rose Tyrien |

| 733 A S3 | 625 B S1 | 660 A S1 | 667 A(iii) S1 | 178 AA S4 | 706 A S3 | 538 A S1 | 322 A(iii) S1 | 621 A S1 | 327 A S2 |
| Winsor Violet (Dioxazine) | Spectrum Violet | Ultramarine | Ultramarine (Green Shade) | Cobalt Blue | Winsor Blue | Prussian Blue | Indigo | Sky Blue | Intense Blue |

| 692 AA S3 | 720 A S3 | 482 A S2 | 484 A S2 | 046 A S1 | 459 A S2 | 483 B S2 | 447 A S2 | 599 A S2 | 369 A S2 |
| Viridian | Winsor Green | Permanent Green Deep | Permanent Green Middle | Brilliant Green | Oxide of Chromium | Permanent Green Light | Olive Green | Sap Green | Linden Green |

| 257 A S1 | 678 A S1 | 507 A S3 | 564 A S1 | 470 A S3 | 554 AA S1 | 676 AA S1 | 609 AA S1 | 076 AA S1 | 505 A S3 |
| Flesh Tint | Venetian Red | Perylene Maroon | Red Ochre | Perylene Violet | Raw Umber | Vandyke Brown | Sepia | Burnt Umber | Perylene Black |

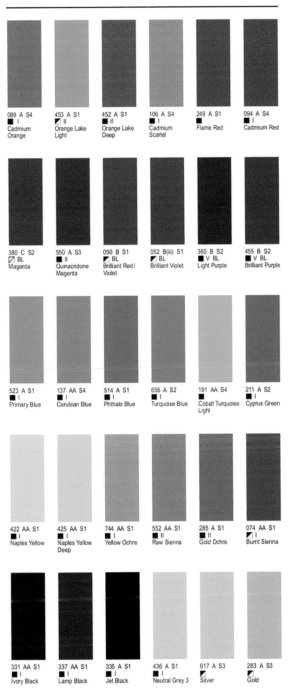

089 A S4
■ I
Cadmium
Orange

453 A S1
◪ II
Orange Lake
Light

452 A S1
■ II
Orange Lake
Deep

106 A S4
■ I
Cadmium
Scarlet

249 A S1
■
Flame Red

094 A S4
■ I
Cadmium Red

380 C S2
◪ BL
Magenta

550 A S3
■ II
Quinacridone
Magenta

050 B S1
◪ BL
Brilliant Red /
Violet

052 B(ii) S1
◪ BL
Brilliant Violet

360 B S2
■ V BL
Light Purple

455 B S2
■ V BL
Brilliant Purple

523 A S1
■ I
Primary Blue

137 AA S4
■ I
Cerulean Blue

514 A S1
■ I
Phthalo Blue

656 A S2
■ I
Turquoise Blue

191 AA S4
■
Cobalt Turquoise
Light

211 A S2
■ I
Cyprus Green

422 AA S1
■ I
Naples Yellow

425 AA S1
■ I
Naples Yellow
Deep

744 AA S1
■ I
Yellow Ochre

552 AA S1
■ II
Raw Sienna

285 A S1
■ II
Gold Ochre

074 AA S1
◪ I
Burnt Sienna

331 AA S1
■ I
Ivory Black

337 AA S1
■ I
Lamp Black

335 A S1
■ I
Jet Black

436 A S1
■ I
Neutral Grey 3

617 A S3
◪
Silver

283 A S3
◪
Gold

designers often confound the purists by combining several different media in one piece of work, frequently working over a painted surface with crayons, coloured pencils, felt-tip pens, and almost anything else that comes to hand. Coloured pencils, either permanent or water-soluble are particularly useful for adding fine details to costume designs, and pastels are also popular with some designers.

What Colours to Buy?

A bewilderingly wide range of colours is available at art stores, but you will certainly not need all of them, even if you could afford to buy the whole range. For a basic palette in Designers Gouache, watercolour or acrylic paints, start your collection by buying two versions of each of the primary colours – one warmer and the other cooler – and also include a couple of browns, blacks and whites. For example:

Reds
Alizarin Crimson (slightly bluish red).
Flame Red (orangey red)

Yellows
Cadmium Yellow (clear, bright yellow)
Yellow Ochre (deep, rather dull yellow)

Blues
Ultramarine (slightly purplish blue)
Prussian Blue (deep, rather greenish blue)

Browns
Burnt Umber (very warm reddish brown)
Sepia (cooler, slightly greenish brown)

Blacks
Ivory Black (good for mixing with other colours to create shades)
Lamp Black (dense, opaque black with good covering ability)

Whites
Zinc White (good for mixing with other colours to create tints)

41

Permanent White (opaque white with good covering ability)

Chinese White ('body' colour for use with watercolours)

With the above selection of colours, you will find you can mix almost any colour you need. However, you will soon find that you develop personal favourites from the other colours in the chart – possibly Bengal Rose (an intense violet-pink), or Viridian Green (a strong bluish green), which are impossible to mix from other colours. A tube of Neutral Grey is also useful for reducing the intensity of strong colours; and everybody's favourite, Payne's Grey, named after the British watercolourist William Payne (1760–1830), who always recommended this particular blended colour to his students. It is a very deep, slate grey that mixes well with other colours. Unfortunately, it is not usually available in gouache, so you may have to resort to buying it as watercolour; this will, however, mix reasonably well with gouache. Greatly diluted, Payne's Grey is excellent for use as a wash when sketching.

BUYING BRUSHES

When looking through the selection of brushes in an art store, you may be horrified at the high cost of the very best sables. This is because they are made from the tail hairs of the Siberian mink, not cut at the end, but set into the ferrule with the naturally tapering ends of the hair forming the point. However, although these expensive brushes are a delight to use, they are an unwise choice for the theatre designer, for we often need to use our brushes in unconventional ways, particularly when painting and texturing set models with destructive substances such as varnishes and plasters, frequently on coarse and unusual surfaces that will quickly ruin a fine-quality brush. Fortunately, there is a wide range of much cheaper brushes available, which are excellent for most jobs. Camel hair brushes (not really made from camels, but merely a name given to a mixture of low-quality hairs) are much cheaper than sable and are good for both costume designs and set renderings. There are also some excellent brushes made from synthetic hair that are even cheaper. The way to test the quality of a brush is to wet the bristles and check that the moistened hairs come to a nice sharp point. (Simply drawing it between your lips is the easy, but far from hygienic, way to do this. Thoughtful art store managers will discourage this practice by placing a glass of water beside their brushes.) Bend the wet bristles by gently pressing them against a convenient surface, and check that they spring back again into their original position when you lift up the brush. If they remain sticking out at a right angle to the handle, you do not want this brush. A good selection of sizes to begin with might be numbers 9, 4, 3, 1, and an extra-thin brush such as 00 for really fine work. Obviously, the thinner the brush, the cheaper the cost. Keep your old, worn brushes to be used for tasks such as rough texturing models or applying varnishes, which you know will probably ruin the brush. It is also a good idea to buy one or two very cheap children's brushes that you can treat as disposable for this kind of job, but beware of loose hairs, which have a tendency to attach themselves to the wet surface, and will leave a mark when pried off.

PRACTICAL EXERCISES

1. **Make your own colour wheel.** First draw the circular outline on card or cartridge paper with a pair of compasses, and divide it into twelve equal segments. Then paint a colour wheel containing primary, secondary and tertiary colours. Use gouache or acrylic colours, and try to achieve a really good balance of the colours, so that each colour lies visually midway in hue between those on either side. Work with care so that the finished wheel looks crisp and well presented.
2. **Colour palette exercises.** Select a coloured photograph from a magazine (*National Geographic* is a good source). Choose one that contains a wide range of colours, but not too

much very fine detail. Lay a sheet of tracing paper over the photograph and trace the outlines of all the main shapes, greatly simplifying the image, and ignoring small details. Using graphite paper, trace off the picture several times onto sheets of cartridge paper or thin card for the following exercises:

- Colour the shapes you have drawn, using the photograph as a reference, but restricting yourself to using only the three primary colours, mixing them together with black and white to obtain an approximation of the colours in the original picture.
- Paint another version, intensifying all the colours as much as possible (that is, without the addition of black or white).

- Paint a version with about 50 per cent neutral grey added to each colour.
- Paint a version with about 50 per cent white added to each colour.
- Choose a primary colour (red, yellow or blue) and paint a version of the picture using only colours mixed from the two other primary colours plus black and white.
- Repeat the last exercise, selecting a different primary colour to omit.
- Repeat again, omitting the third primary colour.

Examine and compare the results: What kind of mood or emotion does each one suggest? Which do you find most pleasing, and why?

Colour palette exercises by Renate Pohl. From top left to bottom right: selected magazine photograph; reproduced with a reduced colour range; with all colours intensified; 50 per cent neutral grey added to all colours; limited palette version with selected primary colour (yellow) omitted.

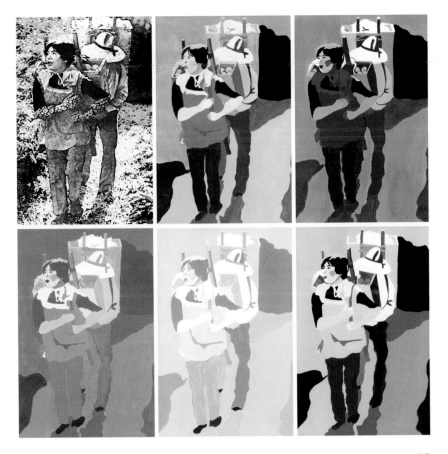

TIMMS CENTRE FOR THE ART

"CRIMES OF THE HEART"
by Beth Henley

3 BASIC DRAFTING TECHNIQUES

> Well, it's back to the old drawing-board.
>
> **Peter Arno, US cartoonist (1904–68)**

Hand-drafting is done on a drawing-board using a straight edge and other instruments as guides. Precision, neatness and a well-ordered approach characterize good drafting, and ideally, no line should be produced without the aid of a guide of some kind. A drawing-board may be a self-standing piece of studio furniture, or the portable type that can be set up on a table and folded away at the end of a work session (*see* page 11). A parallel rule or drafting machine attached to the board is more or less essential for accuracy and speed. You can use a simple T-square, (see illustration), but for accurate results, it needs to be held very tightly against the edge of the board as you draw to avoid slippage, which means that one hand must always be dedicated to controlling the T-square, so the use of other instruments in combination with it can sometimes be difficult.

The drafting machine, invented in 1930, is a much more versatile and accurate drawing aid, providing an easily adjustable straight edge and permitting lines to be drawn at any angle. A good drafting machine is an expensive item to buy, but a cheap one may not produce really accurate work, so can often prove to be a false economy. If funds are limited, it is preferable to buy a parallel rule, which, being much less complicated in construction, is considerably cheaper, and can usually be depended upon to produce accurate results. In fact, the simpler mechanism means that it tends to be more reliable than a drafting machine, and many designers actually prefer it for this reason.

OPPOSITE:
The stage plan compared with the finished set for Crimes of the Heart *by Beth Henley on stage at the Timms Centre for the Arts, Edmonton, Canada.*

RIGHT: *Using a T-square.*

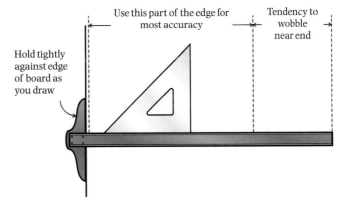

Use this part of the edge for most accuracy

Tendency to wobble near end

Hold tightly against edge of board as you draw

45

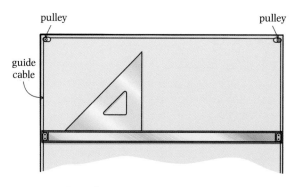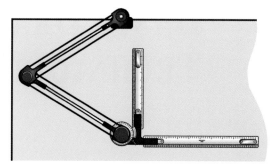

Drawing-boards with parallel rule (left) and drafting machine (right).

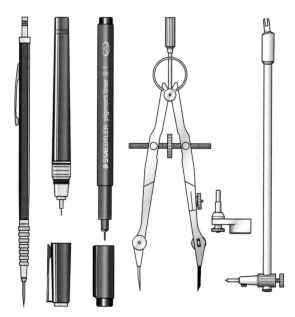

Drafting instruments, left to right: clutch pencil with lead pointer in the cap; ink drafting pen; felt-tip drafting pen; compasses; adapter to fit pen to compasses; extension arm for compasses.

Stencils and other guides for drafting. Top left to bottom right: set-squares; French curves; circle stencil; 360° protractor; wavy line stencil; flexible ruler.

DRAWING INSTRUMENTS

A clutch-type drafting pencil such as the one shown in the illustration above is the best option for technical drawing. Note that the exposed lead needs to be considerably longer for drafting than for sketching, and kept very sharp for accuracy. A lead pointer (such as the one shown on page 21) will not only ensure a really sharp point, but also contains a gadget for maintaining the correct length of lead. If you choose to use a normal wood pencil for drafting, the wood should be shaved back to expose about 1.5cm (½in) of lead. Compass leads are best sharpened to a chisel point with a knife or against fine sandpaper, but need very frequent re-sharpening. (Note the lead in the compasses in the illustration above.) For final drawings, an ink drafting pen such as the one shown gives the very best results, but good results may also be obtained with the much cheaper hard felt-tip type. Note the thin metal tube around the drawing tip, designed to slide along the ruler and keep the tip just clear of the edge. Do not use ordinary felt-tip pens, as the ink will inevitably get onto the edges of your drawing instruments, transfer itself to your fingers and cause indelible smudges on the paper. Note that you need a different size of pen for each line width, for you cannot obtain a thicker line by merely pressing down harder as you can with a pencil. It is possible to produce your final drawings in pencil, but it requires much more time and skill to maintain the differences between several different line-weights, and copy machines often find it difficult to cope with them satisfactorily, for instead of merely copying pure black lines in a variety of thicknesses as in an ink drawing, they must translate a range of grey pencil tones into black printer ink. This usually means that the high setting required to reproduce the faintest pencil lines has a distressing tendency to print a greyish texture over the whole sheet from the off-white tracing paper, and this can make light-weight lines difficult to read. If you intend to have many pencil drawings copied, it is a good idea first to print a test sheet drawn on the same type of paper to establish the kind of line-weights required to produce satisfactory copies.

STENCILS AND OTHER INSTRUMENTS

You will need two pairs of set-squares or triangles – a large pair and a small pair. The set-squares consist of one triangle of 90° × 45° × 45° and another of 90° × 60° × 30°. The larger set-squares tend to give greater accuracy when used against a straight edge, but small ones are useful for finely detailed jobs such as cross-hatching small areas. It is often not realized that a pair of set-squares can be used in combination to produce any angle of 15° increments, as demonstrated in the diagram below.

Set-squares used in combination to produce increments of 15°.

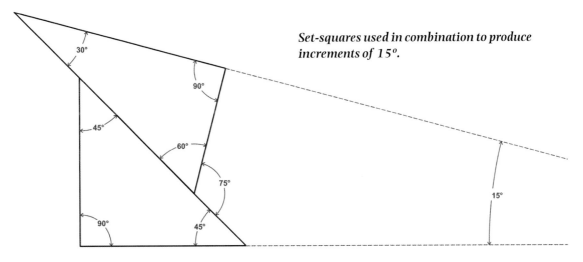

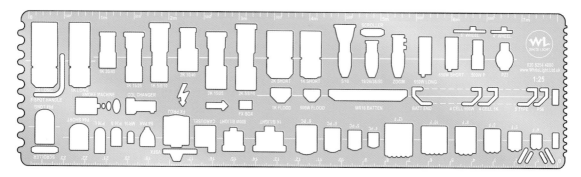

Lighting stencil from White Light Ltd.

A set of French curves, such as the one illustrated on page 46, sometimes known as a Burmester set, will provide a guide for almost any curve you cannot draw with compasses, and a wavy line stencil is particularly useful to set and lighting designers for drawing hanging drapes on stage plans. Lighting designers will also require a stencil containing all the usual luminaires or lanterns ('instruments' in America) for use when drafting lighting plans and sections. These, such as the one from White Light Ltd. illustrated above, are available from most suppliers of stage lighting equipment in 1:25 and 1:50 scales, and contain symbols for almost everything a lighting designer may need, including moving lights, and, in the case of the one illustrated, two handy 'wavy line' stencils. Lighting designers in North America can obtain imperial scale stencils from Field-Templates in New York. (*See* 'Useful Web Sites' at the end of this book.)

A good pair of compasses is more or less essential. Make sure you buy one with a long extension arm for drawing large circles for revolves or the curved edge of an apron stage, and also a little gadget to adapt your drafting pen to the compass arm. Small circles are more conveniently drawn with a circle stencil.

PAPER FOR DRAFTING

Your final drawings will usually be done in ink on tracing paper, produced by tracing off the preliminary drawings, which may also, but not necessarily, be done on the same type of paper.

Standard Paper Sizes

The International Standard ISO 216 is used all over the world, apart from North America and Canada. Paper sizes are classified by numbers with an 'A' prefix, each diminishing size being determined by halving the longer dimension of the size above, thus:

A0	841mm × 1189mm
A1	594mm × 841mm
A2	420mm × 594mm
A3	297mm × 420mm
A4	210mm × 297mm
A5	148mm × 210mm

North America and Canada use a different system referred to as ANSI (American National Standards Institute), but it maintains the principle of halving the longer dimension:

ANSI E	864mm × 1118mm
ANSI D	559mm × 864mm
ANSI C	432mm × 559mm
ANSI B or 'ledger'	279mm × 432mm
ANSI A or 'letter'	216mm × 279mm

Most set drawings at a scale of 1:25 can be made to fit onto an A1 sheet. However, when working on large stages, you may find that the complete stage plan is larger than A1, in which case you must either use an A0 size sheet, or draw the plan at a smaller scale, for example 1:50. In North America, most drawings at 1:24 (or ½in to 1ft) will conveniently fit onto an ANSI D size sheet, but the plans of larger stages may require size ANSI E, or a smaller scale, such as 1:48 or ¼in to 1ft.

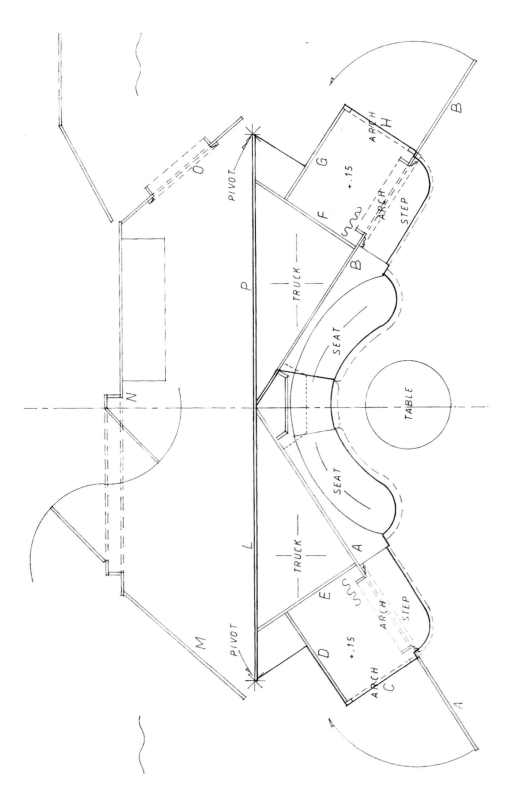

Detail from a hand-drafted stage plan of a touring set for Alan Ayckbourn's evening of one-act plays, Confusions.

Tracing paper is sold either in separate sheets of various sizes, or in rolls. A whole roll of good quality tracing paper may seem rather expensive, but it is, in fact, by far the most economical way to buy it, slicing off sheets with a paper knife as required. Tracing paper is sold by weight (in grams), so you should bear in mind that a roll of thick paper will contain a shorter linear length than a roll of thin paper. A good medium weight paper for general purposes is 90gsm (grams per square metre). The lighter weights are useful for rough work, but tend to be flimsy and tear easily.

The most convenient width to buy is 84.1cm (just over 33in), which is the length of the longer side of an A1 sheet, or the shorter side of an A0 sheet, so both sizes can be cut from the same roll. Tracing paper is an organic material, and like all papers, it will stretch or shrink depending upon the degree of humidity in the air. This is particularly noticeable when a sheet of paper is left taped to the drawing-board overnight, and although beautifully smooth the night before, in the morning is seen to have worrying puckers and cockles caused by a nightly change in humidity.

These distortions will usually vanish again during the day, and generally cause no problem. However, be aware that the length of long lines can be slightly altered by this effect, sometimes causing small inaccuracies. Paper distortion can also be caused by the heat from copying machines, producing slightly inaccurate prints, which is one of the reasons why dimension lines are necessary.

For drawings that are intended to have a long life span, such as the master copies of a theatre's stage plans, which are expected to last for several years, a plastic tracing film that will not tear or distort like tracing paper is a better choice. The plastic film has a slight 'tooth' on the side intended to be used for drawing. Note that ink takes rather longer to dry on tracing film, so special care must be taken to avoid smudging.

THE STAGE PLAN

The stage plan is, perhaps the most significant drawing for any type of show, although it gives little or no impression of how the set will appear to the audience. Basically, it is a map of the stage showing the scenery with the furniture and larger props in their correct positions. Like most maps, it is not intended to show how those objects will appear to the viewer, but merely to indicate their size and relative positions. However, because it precisely defines the space created by the designer for the performers to inhabit, together with its relationship to the architectural structure of the stage and to the audience, the stage plan contains much crucial information. It will probably be the first drawing produced by the designer, and all other technical drawings are in some way related to it. Stage plans are drawn to scale (*see* page 44) and are 'orthographic'. That is, the drawing plane, as represented by the surface of the paper, is always parallel to a major surface of the object being drawn: in the case of a plan, this is the floor.

Orthographic drawings have the advantage that facets are represented without the distorting effect of a perspective drawing, and objects are shown in their true scale-size, shape and proportion. Note that a stage plan is not a 'bird's-eye view' of the set, for any items above floor level would obscure anything beneath them, and no perspective techniques are involved as one might expect in a literal 'bird's-eye view'. It is usually imagined to be drawn at floor level, but if this were strictly true, many details, such as windows or the tops of tables, could not logically be indicated at all, as they do not reach to the floor. Therefore, architects generally visualize a floor plan as a horizontal section, taking a cut through the structure at a fairly arbitrary distance from the floor, but including windows and similar features in the cut, with the parts above the cut removed so that the viewer appears to be looking straight down onto the cut edges of the set at all points. Set designers need to employ a similar technique. Any elements not touching the stage floor, such as pieces hanging above the acting area, or the tops of openings such as doorways and arches are indicated with a 'broken' line, consisting of a row of short dashes. The dashes should always be longer than the spaces between them, and, as a rule of thumb, the higher the element is from the floor, the shorter the dashes should be. Thus, the

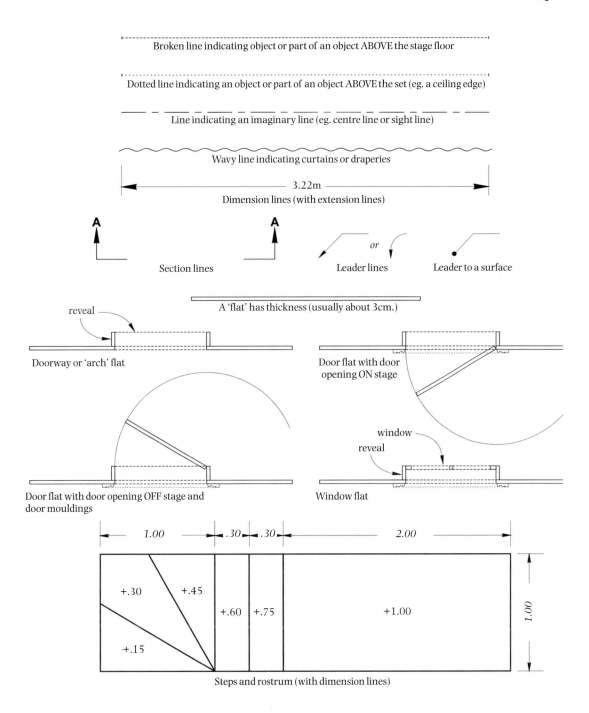

Broken line indicating object or part of an object ABOVE the stage floor

Dotted line indicating an object or part of an object ABOVE the set (eg. a ceiling edge)

Line indicating an imaginary line (eg. centre line or sight line)

Wavy line indicating curtains or draperies

3.22m

Dimension lines (with extension lines)

Section lines   Leader lines   or   Leader to a surface

A 'flat' has thickness (usually about 3cm.)

reveal

Doorway or 'arch' flat

Door flat with door opening ON stage

Door flat with door opening OFF stage and door mouldings

window

reveal

Window flat

1.00   .30   .30   2.00

+.30   +.45

+.60   +.75   +1.00

+.15

1.00

Steps and rostrum (with dimension lines)

Drafting conventions for use on stage plans.

51

Hand-drafted elevation of the Act 2 set for Alan Ayckbourn's Confusions.

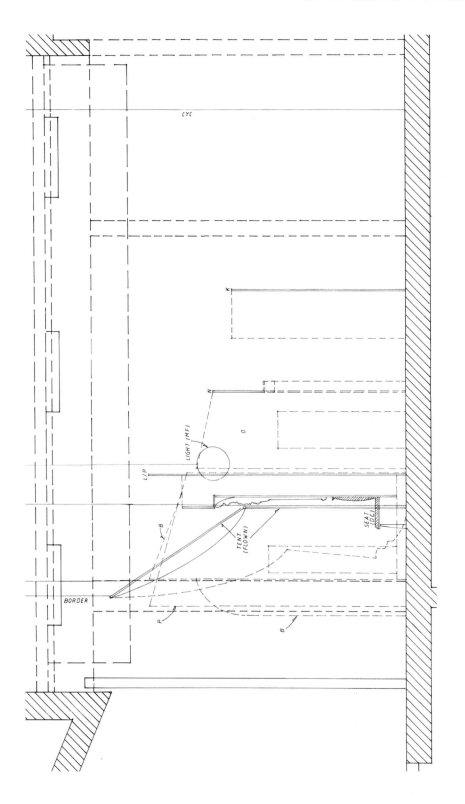

Detail from a hand-drafted composite section of touring sets for Alan Ayckbourn's Confusions.

tops of doorways will be shown with longer dashes than, say, a border hanging high above the set. 'Dotted' lines, consisting of rows of little dots as opposed to dashes, are tedious to draw and are rarely used, but can sometimes be useful for a discreet indication of very high elements. A notable exception to the above remarks are the plans produced by lighting designers. The purpose of these plans is, of course, to show the positions and types of luminaires or lighting instruments, and although most of them hang high above stage level, it would be tedious and confusing to indicate them using broken or dotted lines, for in this case they are the main subject of the drawing. Therefore, it is safe to assume that a lighting plan is drawn from the average level of the lighting bars, so that they may be rendered in solid lines. A simplified version of the set plan, drawn in lines of a much lighter weight, is usually included for guidance.

Remember that flats are usually constructed on a timber frame, and consequently have thickness, usually about 3cm (1¼in), so it is not sufficient to indicate them merely with a single line. (See diagram of drafting conventions above.) The thickness of draperies or painted cloths is minimal, so these may be drawn with a single line, using a wavy line stencil to indicate any drapes with fullness.

ELEVATIONS

These are also orthographic and drawn to scale; however, the drawing plane in this case is vertical.

Most frequently, an elevation shows the front of the set or object depicted, but it can also be drawn from a side or even the back if this is desirable. At first glance, a front elevation often gives the impression of a perspective rendering, but no perspective techniques are involved. For this reason, when labelling drawings, a term such as 'Front Elevation' is preferable to 'Front View', which might suggest a perspective view. However, because of its superficial similarity to a perspective rendering, it has the advantage of giving some indication of how a set will appear to the audience,

which is something a plan cannot do.

SECTION DRAWINGS

The term 'section' here indicates an imaginary 'cutting-through' the set or object depicted. Do not confuse it with the term 'section' meaning 'part of'. Most frequently, the section or 'cut' is taken along the centre line, and the drawing represents what one might see looking towards the imaginary cut edges when the opposite part is removed. A section drawing of the whole stage, showing as much of the auditorium as is conveniently possible, with the set and any masking pieces in their correct positions, is particularly useful to lighting designers. In shows containing a number of flown elements, a section showing sightlines from the front row seats is useful to stage technicians when rigging flying-lines, allowing them to see at a glance the heights required to set borders, and what parts of the space above the set are visible to the audience. Sections are not always taken along the centre line, and are sometimes not even straight. In some cases it is more convenient to make the imaginary cuts elsewhere, depending upon the nature of the set or object depicted. In this case the cut is indicated by a 'section line' labelled 'A–A' etc., the angled arrows at each end indicating the direction of view. (See 'Drafting conventions for use on stage plans' on page 51.)

WORKING DRAWINGS

These are the drawings that the builders will use to construct the set. They are, of course, almost always orthographic and drawn to scale. They should show accurately, and in as much detail as possible, everything that is to be built or pulled from stock. All parts should be clearly labelled and dimensioned. It is usual to label all the pieces of a set with letters running alphabetically from stage right, using the same letters on the plan so that drawings may be easily compared. (The letter 'I' is often omitted to avoid confusion with a short line or the lower-case letter 'l'.) Painted detail is not usually indicated, unless a built object is directly

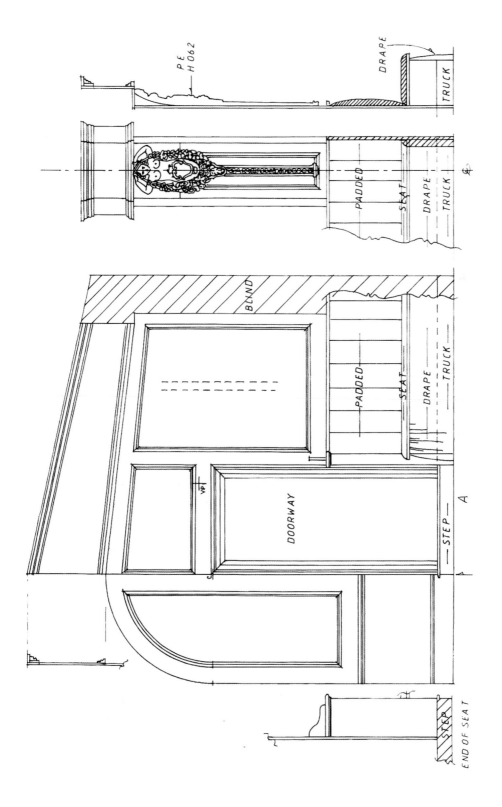

Detail from hand-drafted working drawings for Act 2 of Alan Ayckbourn's Confusions.

related to it, such as the edge of an irregularly profiled flat that must be cut around the outline of the paintwork. It is not necessary for the designer to show exactly how the pieces are to be constructed: the builders probably know much more about this aspect than the designer. If necessary, the Master Carpenter or Head of Construction will make his own construction drawings based upon the designer's drawings. Put simply, the designer draws the scenery from the front, and the builder draws it from the back.

PARALINE AND ISOMETRIC DRAWINGS

All the types of drawing discussed so far are 'paraline' drawings. That is, all parallel lines in the objects depicted remain truly parallel, never converging as they do in a perspective drawing. Most stage sets can be described in this way, using a combination of plan, elevation and section, and items such as props or pieces of furniture can be drawn in a similar manner, although for smaller objects, it is convenient to group all the drawings onto a single sheet, as in the drawing for a hallstand reproduced below. At the right hand side

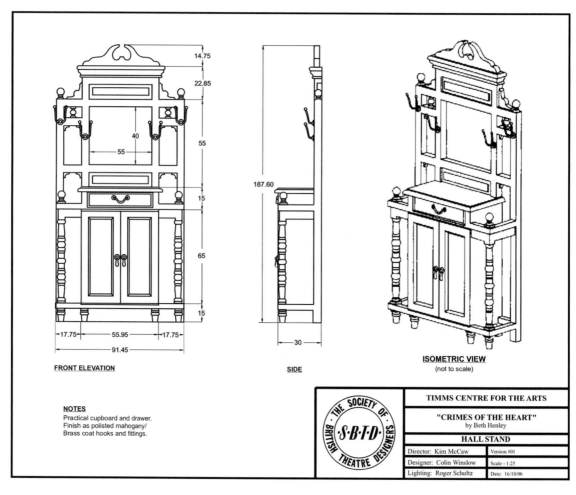

FRONT ELEVATION

SIDE

ISOMETRIC VIEW
(not to scale)

NOTES
Practical cupboard and drawer.
Finish as polisted mahogany/
Brass coat hooks and fittings.

THE SOCIETY OF · S·B·T·D · BRITISH THEATRE DESIGNERS

TIMMS CENTRE FOR THE ARTS	
"CRIMES OF THE HEART" by Beth Henley	
HALL STAND	
Director: Kim McCaw	Version #01
Designer: Colin Winslow	Scale - 1:25
Lighting: Roger Schultz	Date: 16/10/06

Working drawing for a hallstand.

of this sheet is another type of drawing, referred to as 'isometric'. At first glance an isometric rendering gives the impression of a perspective view, but, in fact, it contains no perspective distortion, as all visible surfaces are given equal emphasis. In this case, all the lines representing the horizontal lines of the front and side planes are actually set at 15° to the horizontal. These lines may be set at 30° or 45° to the horizontal suggesting a higher angle of view, or one side may be set at 30° and the adjacent side at 60°, giving more emphasis to one vertical plane than the other. These last two types of drawing would be referred to as 'plan oblique' as they both give greater emphasis to the plan than at the shallower angles. You should choose the type of drawing most appropriate for the object you wish to depict.

WORKING TO SCALE

Unless you are drawing very small props, it is obviously not possible to draw at full size, so all set drawings need to be drawn to scale. The appropriate scale is determined by the size of the objects represented and the size of the sheet they are to be printed on. Nearly all set drawings are made at a scale of 1:25, or twenty-five times smaller than reality, so most sets will fit onto an A1 sheet of paper, or A0 for particularly large stages. This simply means that the actual size of anything drawn on the page can be determined by multiplying by twenty-five. Note that the system of measurement is immaterial here: the scale works whether the drawing has been made using centimetres, inches, cubits or even thumb-joints.

Whichever system you use, multiply by twenty-five to find the full size in the same unit of measurement. North America is now the only country in the world still using the old imperial system of measurement (feet and inches), so the scale used here is normally 1:24 (sometimes expressed as ½in to 1ft), which is a much more convenient scale when counting in 'twelves' rather than 'tens', so if the stated scale is 1:25 or 1:50 it indicates that the draftsman was probably thinking metrically, and if the scale is stated as 1:24 or 1:48 it probably indicates the use of the imperial system. However, if you were to measure a

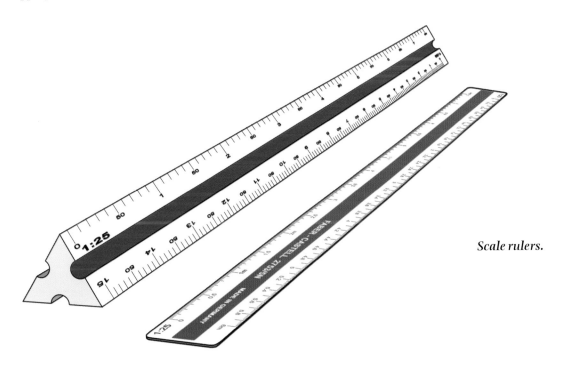

Scale rulers.

1:24 scale drawing in centimetres, you could simply multiply by twenty-four to obtain the result in centimetres (although the calculation may be anything but 'simple'). It is rarely necessary to convert to a different system of measurement. Every sheet of technical drawings should have the scale clearly indicated in the title-box, and any areas not drawn to scale, or drawn to a different scale, should be clearly annotated as such. Avoid the use of '1 = 25' or '½in = 1ft', which, as they are clearly not 'equal', is literal nonsense. The colon is used to indicate a ratio, usually expressed as 'to' when speaking, so scales should always be written as 1:25, 1:24, or ½in to 1ft, etc.

To avoid complicated mathematical calculations when working to scale, a scale ruler should be considered an essential piece of equipment. The scale ruler looks a little daunting at first, particularly to those of us who are not natural mathematicians. However, it is really not difficult to understand: first make sure that you buy one containing the scales you need. 1:25 is the industry standard scale, but sometimes you may need to work at 1:50 to show very large stages at a convenient size, or 1:20 for very detailed drawings.

(1:20 is a very easy scale to use because it is easy to multiply by 20 in your head. However, sheets of drawings can often become inconveniently large when working at this scale.) If you work in North America and need to use the old imperial measurements (feet and inches) you will need to buy a ruler containing scales of 1:24 and 1:48. You will find the scales clearly marked on the ruler near the '0' at the beginning of each scale. Triangular-section rulers like the one illustrated are a good choice, not only because they have more edges than the flat type, and can therefore contain more scales, but also because they are easier to handle and the printed edge is sharper and tilted conveniently towards the drawing. Each side is usually coded with a different-coloured stripe along the centre to make it obvious if you have accidentally changed the side as you work.

Look at the two scales printed below. The top scale (1:25) is the one you will use most frequently when working metrically. The larger figures beneath the scale indicate metres at a scale of 1:25. Between these figures, divisions of half a metre (or 50cm) are indicated with shorter lines. Slightly shorter than these are some lines without

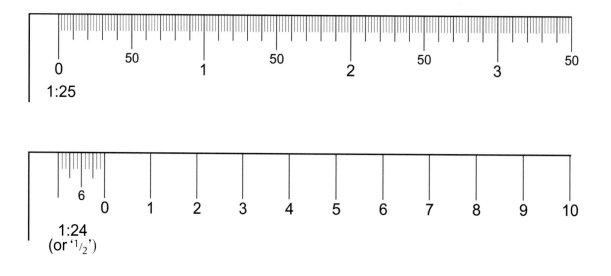

Reading a scale ruler.

numbers, but you can probably work out that they show 10cm divisions, and the shortest lines of all show divisions of just 2cm each. Some rulers show 1cm divisions, but at many scales the thickness of the line alone is about the equivalent of one centimetre, which can make them difficult to read, and it is a simple matter to estimate the midpoint between two of the smallest divisions if you need to measure an odd number of centimetres. The lower scale of 1:24 is the one you will use most if you are working with the imperial measurement system. The larger figures beneath the scale here indicate feet at a scale of 1:24. However, note that these figures do not start right at the beginning of the scale: immediately before the '0' is a series of very small divisions representing inches. The 6in, or ½ft, division is marked with a figure 6. The slightly smaller lines at either side of the 6in division indicate 3in, and the very smallest lines between these indicate 1in divisions. Thus, if you need to mark a line 5' 9' long at a scale of 1:24, you would count off five of the longest lines along the scale, then include nine of the very smallest lines from the divisions before the '0' mark. Other scales work in exactly the same way, although you may find that working with scales smaller than 1:25 the single units are so small that they become impossible to read, and are therefore often indicated in groups for the sake of clarity. Check for this before you begin to draw and carefully count up how many centimetres or inches are represented by the smallest divisions at the scale you are using. It is easy to make mistakes here. Note that your scale ruler may contain some scales starting at the right hand end and reading from right to left, instead of starting at the left and reading from left to right as is more usual. This is done to increase the number of scales the ruler can display. Often the scales starting at the right overlap the ones starting at the left. It doesn't really make much difference in use, but can be a little perplexing if you are not expecting it. If you don't like the idea, look for rules that have just a single scale printed along each edge. Preserve the sharp edges of your scale rulers by always storing them in the plastic cases in which they are sold. This is particularly important if you carry them around

with you in a bag or briefcase. You should not use your scale rulers for drawing lines. They are intended to be used as instruments for measuring, not for drawing, and the edges should be kept as clean and sharp as possible, or they will rapidly begin to lose their precision. In practice, of course, there has never been a designer who has not broken this rule, but it is not recommended by the manufacturers, and really is best avoided.

LETTERING AND LAYOUT

A sheet of technical drawings needs to be laid out so that the information it contains is accessible to the viewer in the clearest possible format. It is, of course, possible to communicate your designs by means of sketches on the backs of beer-mats or similar techniques: it is also possible to extract a decaying tooth with a piece of string tied to a door knob, but you would not expect a professional dentist to use this method. Similarly, the scrappy 'back-of-beer-mat' technique is not a good way to inspire confidence in a designer's professional ability. A well drawn and laid out sheet of drawings shows respect for one's colleagues, and indicates an expectation of a high standard of craftsmanship from those who are to work from them. Indeed, a well-produced sheet of technical drawings can be a beautiful and artistic creation in its own right. On the final, ink version of a sheet of drawings you will need to add text in the form of titles, explanatory notes and dimension-lines. Unfortunately, this usually takes much longer than tracing off all the drawn elements, but is, nonetheless, an essential step. You can use freehand lettering if you have a good steady hand, but remember that its purpose is communication not decoration, so avoid unnecessary flourishes.

Draw horizontal guidelines on the sheet you are tracing from to avoid having to erase them from the final copy and possibly causing damage. The most common error is making the letters far too big: the maximum height of a single stroke letter should be no more than 5 mm (¼in), and most letters should be smaller. Spacing between letters should be consistent for easy reading, but this does not mean leaving exactly the same

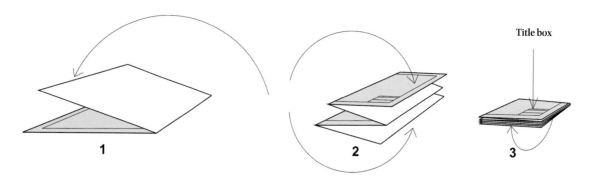

Title box

1   2   3

How to fold a sheet of technical drawings.

amount of vertical space between each letter. For instance, an 'A' followed by a 'V' will need to be set much closer to each other than, say, an 'A' followed by an 'M' to make the area of the spaces between the letters appear equal, regardless of the shape of those spaces. The spacing is always governed by the apparent amount of space, not the actual distance between two letters. All lettering should be horizontal whenever possible, but if it is essential to place any lettering sideways, for good legibility it should always be turned in the same direction, preferably with the bases of the letters towards the right. Lettering stencils such as the one illustrated on page 46 can usually be relied on to produce acceptable lettering. Buy a large one for titles and a smaller one for the rest, but make sure the size of the drafting pen you use is compatible with the size of the letters in the stencil, or it will either be too big to fit through the stencil, or, if too small, the loose fit will create letters consisting of ugly, crooked lines. Compatible pen sizes are usually printed on the stencil. Always use a lettering stencil in combination with the drafting machine or parallel rule on your drawing-board: slide the stencil along the edge to maintain straight lines of text, taking care not to allow the ruler to slip as you work, and paying careful attention to spacing as described above.

It is usual to draw a border around the entire page, setting it at about 1.5cm (½in) from the edge. Use your thickest pen for this. The title-box, drawn with the same line-weight, should be situated in the lower right corner, so that when the sheet is folded in the correct way the box with the information it contains appears on top for easy reference (*see* diagram).

The size of the title-box will depend upon the amount of information it is to contain, but it should probably be not less than about 12cm × 7cm (3in × 5in). Essential items to be contained in the box are:

- Name of the company or venue.
- Name of the show.
- Number of Act and/or scene if appropriate.
- Type of drawing (plan, working drawings, section etc.).
- Scale (this must never be omitted).
- Director's name.
- Designer's name (your own name).
- Names of any other designers involved, such as the Lighting Designer.
- Number of sheet and version number if applicable.
- The date. Always remember to date all your drawings. Occasionally things fall behind in the production process, and it is very easy for the designer (often absent from the post-production post-mortem) to be quite unjustifiably blamed for late submission of designs. The date is your insurance against this.

	NUOVA OPERA 2009		
THE SOCIETY OF · S·B·T·D · BRITISH THEATRE DESIGNERS	**"COSÌ FAN TUTTE"** by Wolfgang Amadeus Mozart		
	STAGE PLAN - Act 2		
	Director: Michael Cavanagh	Scale - 1:25	4 / 16
	Designer: Colin Winslow	Version: #03	
	Lighting: Lee Livingstone	Date: 28/04/09	

Layout of a typical title-box.

The lettering in the title-box can be slightly larger than in the body of the drawing, but never enormous or over-elaborate. A personal or professional society logo can be included if you wish, but do not waste time drawing an elaborate design by hand. You can usually buy an ink-stamp version to print onto hand-drafted sheets. (The title-box and logo in the diagram shown were produced digitally.)

Generally speaking, drawings will initially be made using a fairly hard pencil (say, 2H) and finally traced off in ink to produce clean, crisp copies when printed out at your local copy bureau. Start by drawing the whole set (for a plan), or all the individual parts of the set on separate sheets of paper (for working drawings), using an appropriate scale (usually 1:25). Tape a sheet of paper to the board, of the same size as you intend to use for the finished sheet of drawings (A1 is usually a convenient size). Arrange the preliminary drawings on the sheet and fix them into position with small pieces of drafting tape, carefully aligning the drawing on each piece with the straight edge of your drafting arm or parallel rule. (Note: align the drawing, not the edge of the sheet, as the drawing may not always be precisely aligned to the paper.) Leave enough space between each part for the addition of dimension lines and titles without crowding. If drawing a stage plan, tape your preliminary set drawing into the correct position on a copy of the master plan provided by the theatre. When you are satisfied with the layout, place a sheet of tracing paper over all, taping it down at the corners with drafting tape. (Note: 'drafting' tape is a low-tack version of 'masking' tape. They look the same, but masking tape will almost certainly tear the tracing paper as you remove it, so check the label carefully when buying.) Making a final tracing in ink is a process that is best tackled systematically: start by drawing all the horizontal lines, working down the page from top to bottom. Next draw all the vertical lines, working across the page from right to left. Draw angled lines, then curves and any other irregular lines next, and finish by adding the text. This method of working, particularly important when working on slower-drying, plastic tracing film, will prevent any smudging of the wet ink.

PRACTICAL EXERCISES

1. **Draw a floor-plan.** Draw the plan of a room you know well, such as your bedroom or studio. Use a scale of 1:25 (or 1:24 if working in imperial). Work as accurately as possible, measuring all features carefully, including the thickness of walls, excluding skirting-boards or other mouldings. Include the main items of furniture. If you wish, extend your room plan to cover the entire floor of your house or flat.

2. **Orthographic projections.** Draw orthographic

Twelve Handy Drafting Tips

1. Pull the pencil across the paper when drawing rather than pushing it, allowing it to slope only in the direction in which it is moving. Avoid a tendency to tuck the point underneath the edge of the ruler or stencil.

2. Try to acquire the habit of slightly rolling the pencil between your fingers as you draw to maintain a sharp point.

3. All lines in technical drawings should have a clear start and finish. Never allow them to just taper away at the end. When drawing in pencil, a little extra pressure to define each end of a line is usually sufficient, and in ink, a tiny line drawn at right angles to the line at each end is usual, though note that these termination lines should be very small; certainly no longer than 1mm.

4. When joining a straight line to a segment of a circle or a curve, such as when joining the curve at the top of an arch to the vertical lines at the sides, draw the curved line first then draw the straight lines to it to avoid a visible join.

5. Take care not to leave little gaps where lines are intended to meet at corners of objects. To avoid this, it is common practice to let them just cross each other. However, do not overdo this: it should be hardly perceptible.

6. Line weights should vary depending on the function of the line: the lightest or thinnest lines should be used for dimension lines and 'leaders' (lines linking a title or text note to an object or area in the drawing). Use a fine drafting pen such as a .2mm, or a very sharp, hard pencil such as a 2H for these. Use a .4mm pen or an H pencil for medium-weight lines for general purposes. Heaviest lines from, say, a 1.2mm pen or an HB pencil should be reserved for the sheet border and title-box.

7. Leaders should always be discreet. Avoid showy freehand flourishes that draw the eye and can cause confusion. Use a small arrow at the end of the line just touching the object referred to, or a tiny filled circle placed inside the outline of the object when referring to a surface area.

8. Drafting pens should always be held upright, at 90° to the page in all directions. So when drawing in ink, the drawing-board should not be tilted at more than about 30° to allow a constant flow of ink.

9. Holding the drafting pen upright can be difficult when executing freehand lettering, but a special pen-holder is available from drafting suppliers, with a handle that can be adjusted to a comfortable angle while maintaining the nib in an upright position.

10. When using a lettering stencil, check that your pen size is compatible with the stencil. Each stencil is designed to be used with a specific size of nib, usually printed on the stencil itself.

11. Always wash your hands with soap before starting a final tracing. Greasy fingerprints transferred to the paper as you work can cause the ink to skip.

12. Never stand a cup of coffee or any other drink on your drawing-board. You may think you can avoid spilling it, but this is merely a delusion put into your head by the Drafting Demon, who is always on the lookout for a chance to ruin your work. It will inevitably get tipped over, and hours, or even days of work can be ruined in an instant.

projections of a piece of furniture in your house. If this is your first attempt, choose something fairly simple such as a kitchen chair or cabinet. Include the plan, front and side views at a scale of 1:25 (or 1:24 if working in imperial).

3. **Isometric and plan oblique drawings.**
   a) Using the same object as in the previous exercise, construct an isometric rendering based on equal angles of 30° to the horizontal.
   b) Construct a plan oblique of the same object using axes at unequal angles of 30° and 60° to the horizontal.

4 THEATRICAL MODEL-MAKING

... when they come in to model Heaven ... how they will wield
The mighty frame, how build, unbuild, contrive
To save appearances.
John Milton (1608–1674)

It will be seen from the previous chapter that although technical drawings are indispensable to theatre technicians, to gain a really clear impression of what the set designer has in mind requires a considerable effort of the imagination involving comparison of plans, elevations, working drawings and sections, and unfortunately, not all the people involved in a production have that kind of technical expertise or are willing to devote the amount of time and effort required. The director and cast, among others, also need to know what the finished set will look like on stage, and actors particularly should not be expected to possess a great deal of technical sophistication. Colour is also a vital issue: the lighting and costume designers will be greatly interested in this particular aspect, and the technical drawings give no indication of it whatsoever. The designer can, of course, produce a coloured set rendering of the kind shown below,

OPPOSITE: *Once a production has opened, the set model has lost its reason for existence, and however much work went into their construction, old models usually end their days slowly disintegrating on a storeroom shelf.*

RIGHT: *Set rendering for* A Touch of Purple *at the Thorndike Theatre, Leatherhead.*

65

and if he is a reasonably skillful artist, it can look impressive, but a painted picture of a set design can be as deceptive as a painted portrait, and it is easy for a designer to introduce a considerable amount of wishful thinking into a set rendering, often quite unintentionally. An accurate scale model, on the other hand, can show not only what a completed set will look like when viewed from the auditorium, but also the off-stage spaces surrounding and above it in a way that is clear to even the most uninitiated viewer. The completed final model is an accurate three-dimensional, fully coloured and textured representation that differs from the set as it will appear on stage in one aspect only: size. By means of the model, the director can plan the production in as much detail as he wishes; the actor can see the world he is to inhabit on stage, and note any hazards it may present such as steps, rostra or rakes; the lighting designer can easily assess the best positions to rig lanterns; the costume designer can quickly appreciate the most appropriate colours to use; stage crew can plan scene changes; set builders can check any aspects that may need special treatment and scene painters can use it to mix their colours. All this, of course, is only possible if the model is built as accurately as possible in every respect, so the designer will often find that most of the time spent working on the designs for a show is expended on building and painting the model. How long it takes depends, of course, upon the complexity of the design and the speed at which you work, but as a rule of thumb, having made a careful estimate of the length of time the model will take to construct, you should always multiply the result by at least three to obtain a more accurate estimation.

Presentation set model for Act 1 of NUOVA's production of **La Périchole** *by Jacques Offenbach.* *Photo: Josiah Hiemstra.*

Preliminary sketch model for **What the Butler** *Saw by Joe Orton.*

The very detailed, accurate type of model described above is often referred to as the 'presentation model'. However, designers will often make rough, rapidly constructed white card models or part models before beginning the final version, rather as we sometimes make rough sketches before beginning the final rendering of a set or costume design. These sketch-models can be very useful aids in visualizing the stage-space in three dimensions, particularly during early discussions with the show's director. You will probably need to make rather brutal adjustments with a pair of scissors during these discussions, so do not waste a great deal of time and effort on the sketch model: it is merely the three-dimensional equivalent of a back-of-beer-mat sketch. Some bold sketched outlines on scrap card, cut out with scissors and stuck together with Sellotape is usually all that is required. A collection of model furniture saved from old set models, or cheap plastic pieces bought in toy shops, to place around

the sketch model can also be useful at this stage.

A 'chicken or egg' situation arises here: how can a designer make a model before producing plans and working drawings to establish precisely the form the model is to take? But, on the other hand, if the model is a necessary aid to fully visualizing a set, would it not be better to build the model first, then produce the technical drawings based on the model? The answer is really a matter of personal preference. However, as pointed out above, a presentation model takes a great deal of time and effort to make, so it is advisable to make sure that everything is worked out in detail before beginning and avoid having to make time-consuming alterations at a later stage. Producing plans and working drawings before starting the presentation model has other advantages. The set can be costed from the drawings, and, if necessary, construction can be started before completion of the model. This means that the model may not be completed before the first production meeting, which usually takes place long before the first rehearsal and the formal presentation of the finished model. However, the technical drawings will have been already circulated and, with careful timing, it may be possible to show the white-card model at a first production meeting, even in an incomplete condition. A further advantage to the designer when building a model from the completed technical drawings, is that any small errors or inaccuracies that may have crept into them will be discovered by the designer during construction of the model and can be corrected long before they are incorporated into the actual set, thereby not only saving face, but probably time and money too.

BUILDING MODELS TO SCALE

Having a completed set of technical drawings before starting the final, presentation model can be a great practical help in model construction,

especially if, as is usually the case, the scale selected for the model is the same as that of the drawings. A copy of the stage plan can then be glued to the base board for accurate positioning, and the working drawings traced off to card with graphite paper, or even mounted directly onto the card to be cut out and used in the model. The best way to do this is to use a spray adhesive such as 3M Spray Mount, which will neither distort the paper nor warp the cardboard. Never attempt to mount large sheets of paper to card using a PVA adhesive, as it will inevitably soak into both the paper and the card and cause disastrous cockling and curling as it dries. When using this technique, the drawings need to be very securely fixed to the card and baseboard to avoid any possibility of them lifting when the model is painted. The usual scale for set models is 1:25 (or 1:24 if working in imperial). This scale is convenient for the inclusion of most small details, and produces a model large enough to present to a sizeable group of people. Sometimes,

Simple scale figures cut from card.

68

when working on very large stages, a smaller scale may be preferable, but it is obviously a great convenience to build the model to the same scale as the working drawings, and avoid the necessity of converting from one scale to another. Whatever scale you are using, it is a great help to keep a human figure at the same scale on your work table so that you have a visual reference of the scale constantly available to stand in the partly built model and check for errors of scale. Model shops stock scale figures at most scales intended for use in architectural models, but a simple sketch figure cut from a scrap of waste card can be just as effective. Some model-makers like to make beautifully modelled characters from the show being worked on and present them with the model.

These are very attractive, but it is a time-consuming task, and a far quicker technique is to make a copy of a costume design reduced to the correct scale using a scanner, print it onto card stock, then cut it out and glue a small cardboard strut at the back to support it when standing.

MATERIALS FOR BUILDING SET MODELS

The basic building material is usually cardboard. This, of course, is a generic term that encompasses a wide range of paper-based boards in an equally wide range of thicknesses, which can often make selecting the ideal board a perplexing task.

Cardboard is generally manufactured by gluing together several layers of paper to achieve the thickness required. Cheap cardboard has the annoying habit of separating as you work, especially when cut into very small pieces, and often has poor quality card in the centre layers, which can create untidy or discoloured cut edges, so it is always worth buying the best quality available for a presentation model.

Mount-board
Also known as 'mounting board' or 'matt board', this will probably be the kind of board you use most frequently for set models. As the name suggests, it is designed to be used for making picture-mounts, so it is available in a wide range of colours, usually coloured on one side and white on the other. A black/white mount-board is particularly useful for set models, as the black side can be used to make standard black masking.

Mount-board is usually sold in A1 sized sheets, and varies in thickness depending upon the make and quality, but is usually just over 1mm thick. It will become a little bit thicker if a sheet of working drawings is layered onto it as suggested above. Thus, at the scale of most set models, it represents a thickness of about 4cm (about 1½in) in reality, which conveniently approximates to the thickness of a standard flat. Always check the thickness of the card you are using and remember to allow for it when joining at corners with an overlap.

Other Types of Card
There are a great many other kinds of cardboard available with names such as 'art board', 'museum board', and 'ticket card'. The names actually mean very little, as they are used inconsistently between different manufacturers. However, you will need a range of good quality thinner cards with a reasonable, non-shiny surface for painting. Card is usually designated by the number of layers used to make the card, and two-, three-, four-, or five-sheet cards are generally available. It is helpful to buy a range of thicknesses from the same manufacturer, so you can depend upon them taking paint in the same way. Some makes of card are much more absorbent than others, and this can cause unexpected colour changes as paint dries on them.

Printer card stock is particularly useful, as it has a good surface for painting, and is thin enough to be used in most desk-top printers.

Foam-core Board
This is a board made from polystyrene foam layered between sheets of stout paper. It is very lightweight, and is available in a range of thicknesses from about 2mm–12mm. Black foam-core board, with black polystyrene inside to show black edges when cut, is particularly useful for the construction of model boxes.

Wood

There is a common misconception that the best kind of wood for making models of any kind is balsa. In fact, this is an extremely unsatisfactory wood for making set models: its coarse, loose grain makes it hard to cut accurately, and its extreme absorbency makes it difficult to paint. Fortunately, there is a wide range of other woods available to model-makers which are much more suitable. The most popular of these are obeche and bass woods, both of which have a very close, straight grain, and are sold in model shops as strips or thin planks in the same way as balsa wood. Good model shops will also stock a range of other woods such as mahogany, ash or walnut, which can be used for special finishes.

Plastic and Metal

Most model shops stock a range of very accurately produced plastic and metal strips, rods, tubes and thin sheets for model-making, which can be useful, but sometimes a little difficult to work with. Particularly useful, however, are the pre-constructed architectural parts such as railings, steps, ladders, and a good range of scale furniture from Plastruct Inc. in the USA. Unfortunately, they are available only in imperial scales, but 1:24 is so close to 1:25 that the very small difference is usually acceptable. Many UK model shops sell Plastruct products, but you can also buy them online from www.plastruct.com.

Some useful plastic and metal items available from model shops.

ADHESIVES

PVA (PolyVinyl Acetate)
Usually known as 'white glue', this is the most popular kind of glue among model-makers. It is water based, so it can easily be thinned when needed, and any drips can be cleaned up with a moistened cloth or cotton-bud before they set. Once dry, the bond is fast and waterproof. Do not buy the 'safe' glues intended for use in schools, as they are usually heavily diluted and often do not provide a really strong bond. A thick, smooth consistency that sets rapidly is best for model-making.

Synthetic Resin Glue
Known as 'universal' or 'all-purpose' glues (e.g. UHU or Bostik), these will stick most materials effectively. They begin to set almost immediately on contact, which can be a great time saver, but can prove inconvenient when attempting to reposition a trickily situated item. They are waterproof, and dry transparent, but can be a little difficult to paint over if this becomes necessary. Most synthetic resin glues give off fairly unpleasant fumes, so always use them in a well-ventilated area, and avoid breathing in the fumes directly.

Plastic Cements
As the name suggests, these adhesives are intended specifically for use with plastic, and most of them will not adhere effectively to any other material. They are usually available in two forms, either as a viscous glue such as Revel! Professional Plastic Cement, sold in tubes with a fine needle applicator, or as a thin, clear liquid, such as Plastiweld, which is sold in small jars with a little brush to apply the glue to the joint. These types of glue dissolve a little of the surface of the plastic to produce a weld. Both types dry very rapidly, but give off unpleasant fumes, so always use them in a well-ventilated area and avoid breathing in the fumes directly.

Superglues
This range of adhesives produces an extremely strong, almost instant bond, which might be considered 'overkill' when used in models for the theatre, but cyanoacrylate, the active ingredient on which most of them are based, can be particularly useful for strengthening very delicate parts such as the model railings in the illustration below. Buy the thinnest liquid type for this, and very carefully dribble the glue over the part suspended over a disposable plastic cup to collect the drips. Do not attempt to paint it on: the only result will be a brush firmly and immovably glued

Delicate ironwork railings cut from thin card and strengthened with cyanoacrylate. (10p coin included for size comparison.)

to the model. Cyanoacrylate is a dangerous substance that gives off very noxious fumes. It must always be used in a well-ventilated area (or in the open air, if that is not possible), and a disposable face-mask should be worn. Never attempt to use it without a solvent at hand, preferably one sold by the manufacturer, but in an emergency, nail varnish remover can be an effective alternative. However much care you take, you will inevitably get some on your fingers occasionally, and this means that anything you touch immediately afterwards will become firmly welded to your skin. You have been warned!

TOOLS FOR MODEL-MAKING

The model-maker's most important tool is his cutting knife. Rough cutting can be done with scissors, but they can never produce the clean cuts and high degree of accuracy needed when building a presentation model. Many types of craft knife are available, but most model-makers prefer a scalpel such as those illustrated below for really fine work. They are sold at most craft shops and art stores, with various types of handle and several types of blade. Choose the handle that feels most comfortable in your hand, but whichever you choose, make sure the blade is one that tapers to a sharp point like those in the illustration.

Buy a large number of replacement blades. For really accurate cutting, the blade must be extremely sharp, and cutting cardboard, especially foam-core board, will rapidly remove the sharp edge, creating a tendency to tear rather than cut, so blades should be replaced very frequently. It is economical to work with two knives, reserving one with a really keen blade for finely detailed work, and the other for rough cutting, when a high degree of accuracy is not so important.

Cutting Mat

A vinyl cutting mat is an essential piece of equipment for model-making. They are, to some extent, 'self-healing', which means that straight cuts at 90° to the surface tend to close up again.

Unfortunately, theatrical model-makers frequently need to make angled and other kinds of irregular cuts, that will eventually remove small slices from the surface of the cutting mat, so be sure to buy a double-sided mat, so you can reserve one side for work you know will damage the surface, keeping the other side reasonably smooth and intact. It is not necessary to buy a huge cutting mat – A2 (42cm × 59.4cm, or about 16½in × 23½in) is a suitable size for most jobs. An emergency substitute for a cutting mat is a piece of thick strawboard, such as the back of an old sketchbook, but do not be tempted to use a sheet of plywood, as the grain has an annoying tendency to divert the blade when cutting.

Cutting Rule

Most lines you cut when making set models will be straight, so a metal straight edge to use as a guide is

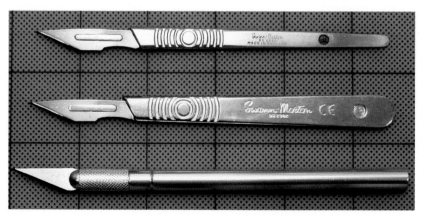

Knives suitable for model-making. Top and middle: Swann-Morton surgical scalpels with #10A blades. Bottom: X-Acto #1 craft knife with #11 blade.

Metal cutting rulers. Top: engraved steel ruler. Middle: cork-backed ruler (showing back). Bottom: aluminium ruler with steel edge and non-slip back.

essential. Never try to cut against a plastic or wooden ruler – the resulting cuts will not be truly straight and the edge of the ruler will rapidly be ruined. Metal rulers specifically designed as cutting guides are available from art stores, incorporating various non-slip devices, such as those illustrated below.

HOW TO CUT CARD REALLY ACCURATELY

Do not attempt to cut through card with a single stroke unless the card is very thin. Several strokes made along the same cut, will produce a much cleaner edge with no tearing. However, great care must be taken to maintain the blade at 90° to the cutting surface with each stroke, or a messy edge

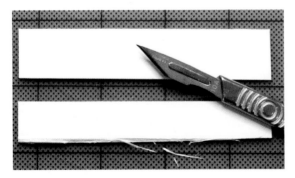

Examples of good (top) and bad (bottom) cuts.

with thin slivers of card hanging from it will be the result. Press down really hard on the metal ruler to prevent it from slipping, and keep your fingers well back from the edge or you run the risk of cutting them. Apart from the fact that a full complement of fingers will be required to complete the model, blood-spots on cardboard can be difficult to paint over. In a similar vein, try to avoid running your finger along newly cut edges, which can easily cause bloody paper cuts.

Cutting Curves

Gadgets for cutting circles are sold in many art stores, but are really only effective when cutting through paper or very thin card. When cutting circles or curves from thicker card, such as mount-board, it is best to work free-hand. Begin by making a very shallow cut, carefully following the marked-out line, and rotating the board as you cut. Keep the blade almost upright so the cut is made using just the point rather than the full length of the blade, which will have a tendency to force the blade into a straight line rather than allowing it to follow a smooth curve. When this first, shallow cut has been completed, carefully following the line, make a second cut a little deeper. The first cut will act as a guide, and the blade will tend to follow along it.

Subsequent strokes can be made with more pressure, as by this time there will be a fairly deep cut to guide the blade.

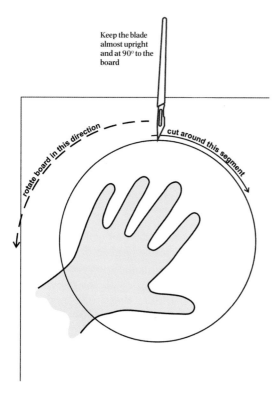

Keep the blade almost upright and at 90° to the board

rotate board in this direction

cut around this segment

Cutting a circle from mount-board.

CUTTING WOOD

Thin planks of wood can be cut with a knife in the same way as mount-board, but accuracy is a little trickier to maintain, as cutting against the grain of the wood can sometimes be difficult, often requiring considerable pressure; and cutting with the grain, although comparatively easy, can sometimes cause the blade to veer away from the intended line to follow the grain instead. To make accurate cuts, slice gradually through the wood in several passes, taking particular care always to keep the blade at 90° to the surface to avoid an angled cut. Cutting irregular shapes from wood is best done with a small electric saw, such as the one illustrated. This is an expensive piece of equipment to buy, but can really speed up the model-building process when working with wood. As with cutting knives, an electric saw needs a really sharp blade to

work efficiently, so lay in a good supply of replacement blades. Wood strips are best cut with a model-maker's saw and mitre-box to ensure a clean, accurate cut. The one illustrated has a small flange underneath which fits against the edge of a table to hold it firmly when in use, and uses a deep saw blade fitted into a standard X-Acto craft-knife handle. It will cut at 90° or 45° angles.

Adjustable models are available that are designed to cut at whatever angle may be set by the user, but these tend to be a little unreliable. Dolls' house suppliers sell miniature architectural features such as mouldings, balusters, door knobs etc., but unfortunately, the usual dolls' house scale is 1:12 (1in to 1ft), which is about twice as big as the scale normally used for set models. However, some of these items can be adapted: wooden ceiling mouldings, trimmed and cut to size with a saw and mitre-box, can make excellent door mouldings; spindles intended for staircases can be used for balustrades, and tiny dolls' house drawer knobs often make good door knobs. It's worth keeping a small stock of these useful items.

A handy scroll-saw for model-making by Proxxon.

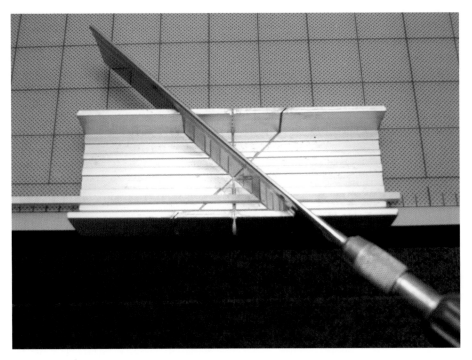

Cutting a wood strip with an X-Acto model-maker's saw and mitre-box.

THE WARP FACTOR

Cardboard is an excellent material for building set models, but has a serious inherent failing: owing to its layered-paper structure, any water-based paint or glue applied to one side of the card will tend to expand the top paper layer on that side, and the card will be forced to bend in compensation. Once a warp has occurred, it is very difficult to persuade the card to lie flat again. You can leave it under a pile of heavy books for days, but usually it will gradually resume its warp when released from pressure. This tendency can be annoying at best, and totally disastrous at worst, so it is important to take steps to counteract its effect when building set models. It is, of course, the water contained in the paint or adhesive that causes the warpage, so it is sometimes possible to limit the effect by painting the back of the card with water immediately after painting the front, then allowing it to dry flat,

thereby causing the card to pull in both directions at the same time, counteracting the warp effect.

However, whenever possible, strengthening strips should be applied in a grid formation to the back of any large pieces during construction. Strips of mount-board glued on edge, as in the illustration on page 76, are generally far stronger than wood strips, which will merely bend with the warp. Avoid using too much water-based glue when applying the strips, as this can also soak into the card and cause warping. This type of strengthening technique is particularly important when building model platforms or rostra, as these pieces usually have to support other set elements, so need to be sturdily built. A rostrum top supported by just cardboard strips around the sides will work only on the very smallest structures, and it is far easier to tackle the problem at the construction stage than to attempt to correct it later when the underside may be inaccessible.

Preventing warp. Back of a model flown piece showing card strips applied for strengthening, and to form reveals around any edges visible to the audience. The bottom left corner is required to fit against a low platform, so is left free.

BENDING CARD AROUND CURVES

It is often necessary to bend a strip of card around a curve to form the side of a curved step or rostrum, or the reveal around the inside of an arch. Thin card can be easily curled by drawing it over the edge of a ruler, but thicker card such as mount-board needs special treatment to produce a smooth curve. The warp factor can actually be useful here, for painting one side of the card with water will often produce a suitable curve. However, bending mount-board around a curve means that the layers on the outside of the curve must stretch to accommodate the extra length, or the layer on the inside must compress, usually resulting in ugly creasing and cockling. To avoid this, make a series of parallel cuts part-way through the card, at right angles to the direction of the curve, on the side that is to be the outside or convex side of the curve, and the card should bend reasonably smoothly. This works fine if the cuts finish up on the back of the model, as in the reveal to an arch, but if it is necessary to show the scored side of the curve, it is best to glue a strip of paper over it when the piece has been glued in position to conceal the cuts. Cut the paper strip slightly too wide, glue it firmly into position, then trim off the excess paper with a scalpel for a neat fit.

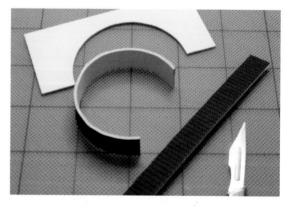

Bending card around a curve.

76

Applying glue from an up-turned teacup.

APPLYING ADHESIVES

Glue is messy stuff, and if allowed to encroach on areas of a model where it is not required, can have a disastrous effect on its finished appearance, so steps must be taken to control this essential, but potentially destructive, substance. Never attempt to squirt adhesive directly from its tube onto pieces of the model. Instead, first squeeze a little of the glue onto a suitable shallow container such as a plastic lid, or the indented bottom of an upturned teacup, and transfer the glue to where it is needed with the point of a cocktail stick or a pointed sliver of card.

You will need to work quickly, especially when applying glue to a large area, or the glue will begin to set before the piece is placed in position. Hold it in position for a few seconds to allow the glue to 'grab', then put the piece aside to allow it to set fully. Synthetic resin glues have a particularly fast 'grab', but PVA glues take a little longer. Some joints may be reinforced by running a little adhesive along the back of the joint, but avoid getting glue on the front of the model at all costs.

Some model-makers like to apply glue from a syringe, and model shops sell small plastic syringes specially produced for this purpose, but it is also possible to modify cheap, disposable hypodermic syringes bought from your local chemist. These can then be used to apply a tiny amount of glue to a very precise location when this is required. The needles are sold separately from the syringes, and you will need considerably more of them than the syringes themselves, so buy several at a time, and note that they are colour-coded to indicate thickness, so you can select the thickness most appropriate for the job in hand. For all but the most detailed work, the thickest needles (usually colour-coded white) work best. The needles have an extremely sharp slanting point which you will need to cut off completely with wire cutters, then carefully tap in a large headed pin to reopen the tiny tube which will have been squashed together in the process. Dispose of the cut-off needle-point carefully: it can be dangerous if left lying around.

Keep the pin to use as a stopper to prevent the glue from hardening in the needle when not in use. Fit the needle onto the end of the syringe, remove the plunger, and squirt in the glue. Then replace the plunger, turn the syringe point up, and drive out the air bubble by depressing the plunger. Your glue dispenser is now ready for use. A syringe filled with glue will remain usable for quite a long time if care is taken to insert the pin when not in use, and can be a handy item to include in a travelling emergency repair kit when transporting models by public transport. However, personal experience has shown that it is not a good idea to carry it with you when travelling by plane, as few security officers will believe your perfectly innocent explanation.

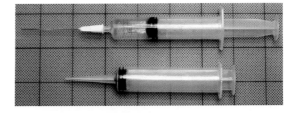

Syringes used to apply glue. Top: disposable hypodermic syringe with needle trimmed to remove point. Bottom: plastic syringe from an art store.

MODELLING ARCHITECTURAL FEATURES

Much of the set designer's work, regardless of individual style, is rooted in architecture, whether this is realistically represented or not. Fortunately, miniature architectural features lend themselves well to construction from cardboard and wood.

Appropriate dolls' house mouldings trimmed to size are often useful, but if these are not available, chair rails, skirting boards, picture rails and plaster mouldings can be built up from strips of card glued together. Recessed panelling can be made by cutting out the panels from the surface card, and gluing extra pieces of card behind in the manner described for panelled doors below.

Doors

Doors should be made to open on set models, for the way the door is hinged is significant on stage, and actors and directors will need to know this

Making a panelled door.

when rehearsing entrances and exits. Start by cutting the door-opening from the cardboard wall, and glue a strip of card of an appropriate width to the back to form the reveal. As most stage scenery walls are in reality only 3 or 4cm thick, reveals are important to suggest a realistic thickness for a set wall. Reveals run vertically down each side of the opening, and also along the top, joining the two side reveals together. Bearing in mind the problem of warping discussed above, it can often be helpful to extend the side reveals right up the back of the cardboard wall so they can perform the additional function of helping to strengthen the piece.

Doors can be built up from layers of card, as shown in the illustration. If both sides of the door are seen by the audience, then you may need to use the same treatment on the back also. Use very thin card for this, or your door will end up impossibly thick. The door can be hinged into the opening in the wall with a strip of paper glued down the side of the door, and down the edge of the wall, or to the back of the reveal, depending on the direction in which the door opens. You may have to trim the door a little to make it fit smoothly, and glue a slim strip of wood or card to the reveal around the inside of the doorway to act as a door stop, to prevent the door from being pushed right through the reveal, breaking the paper hinge. The architrave mouldings cut from wooden dolls' house mouldings, or built up from cardboard strips glued around the door opening, are often useful to conceal the edge of the strip of paper hinge. Finally, fit door handles bought from dolls' house suppliers or made from the cut-off tops of round-headed pins. Door handles on set models seem to hold a peculiar attraction, and it's a safe bet that someone will be unable to resist the temptation to see if they really work, so glue them very firmly into place.

Windows

Making windows in set models seems to create a good deal of anxiety on the part of inexperienced model-makers, and it is true that they usually demand a little extra care and attention. Most windows fall into one of two basic types: the casement window, which opens like a door, hinged at one side, or the sash window, which opens by

Completed model door hinged into flat.

sliding sections of the window frame up and down in a groove. In set models, it is useful to hinge casement and French windows to open in the right direction, as with doors. However, there is little point in attempting to build practical sash windows, as there can be no doubt about which way they will open, and it is difficult to make a delicately cut cardboard window frame run smoothly in a tiny groove. Cutting out panes from cardboard windows can be tricky, but do not attempt to build the window from thin strips of wood, as the very precise cutting and alignment required means that this technique hardly ever works effectively. Do not use card that is too thick: a really good quality card, somewhat thinner than mount-board, works best. Carefully mark out the entire window on the card, and cut out all the panes before cutting around the outside of the frame, so the surrounding extra card can support the frame while the panes are being cut out. The tricky part is cutting right into the corners of each pane, without slicing through the glazing bars. To do this, use a very sharp blade, beginning each cut by carefully inserting the point neatly into the

corner of the pane, and then cutting away from the corner towards the opposite corner. This technique works well for the corner you start from, but it is

Model windows.

really difficult to cut right into the opposite corner, as the blade is naturally pointing in the wrong direction. The way to deal with this is to stop cutting just before you reach the opposite corner, then turn the card around so you can repeat the process along the same cut, but again cutting away from the corner. Work logically down the card as you cut: starting at the top edge of the top left pane, make all the partial horizontal cuts travelling down the window from top to bottom. Then rotate the card through 180° and make all the horizontal cuts from the opposite corners, making sure the blade travels precisely along the partial cuts already made. After cutting all the horizontal lines, rotate the card through 90° and cut all the vertical sides of each pane in the same way. As you cut, the thin glazing bars will have more and more strain put upon them, so leave all the pieces of card you have cut out of the frames in position to give support until all the cutting is complete. Then, finally, cut around the outside of the frame, knock out all the cardboard panes you left in place for temporary support, and admire your skilful handiwork. Casement windows can be hinged with strips of paper in the same way as doors (see above). Remember that sash window frames need to be made to overlap each other by the depth of the topmost horizontal stile of the frame.

Steps and Staircases

Single steps can be constructed in the same way as model rostra or platforms, and irregularly shaped step units are best made as a series of stacked-up shallow rostra. Longer flights of steps or staircases can be built using 'stringers', a technique builders use when building full-size staircases. 'Stringers' are supports specially cut to fit underneath the steps, linking them all together and holding the treads and risers in position. They are usually used in pairs, one at each side of the step unit. Start by marking out the lines where the stringers are to run on a plan of the steps and, taking measurements from the plan, draw up each stringer in scale, remembering to allow for the thickness of the card to be used for the treads and risers. Curved flights of stairs can also be built using this technique, but as the width of the treads along the stringers will vary depending upon where they fall in relation to the curve, marking out the stringers needs very careful attention to achieve a good fit. Open-tread stairs can be created by simply omitting the risers.

Banisters and Balustrades

These are the most fiddly parts to make when building model steps, and as they tend to be rather delicate, it is important that they are fixed in place as firmly as possible so that all your hard work doesn't simply fall apart at the touch of a clumsy finger. The materials you use will depend upon the nature of the design. If the banisters are simply straight, thin strips of square section model-makers' wood, or lengths of very small diameter dowel serve well, but for turned spindles, it is best

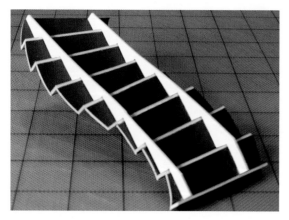

Model steps showing stringers set beneath.

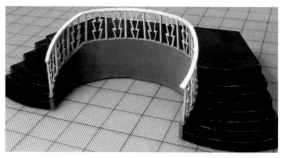

Model banisters. The straight pieces are cut from thin strips of obeche wood, and the 'lightning-strike' art deco pieces are cut from card of a similar thickness.

to start by finding out if suitable pieces are available from dolls' house suppliers or model shops. Shops that sell parts for building model ships often stock beautifully turned miniature balusters and spindles for use on model galleons. If you have to build them from scratch, you will need to employ a little ingenuity. Model-makers' lathes are available, but the degree of precision involved in their manufacture makes them very expensive to buy, and considerable skill and patience is required to use them, especially if you are turning a large number of identical spindles to line a period staircase. Perhaps the simplest technique is to use beads threaded on a wire, mixing beads of different types together in imitation of turned spindles. Thin strips of paper or button thread rolled around the wire to build up the desired shape and thickness, then painted with glue to fix, can be very effective.

Craft shops usually stock a very wide range of beads of all shapes and sizes, and it is useful to lay in a stock of these inexpensive items. When you have discovered the best arrangement of beads, make it permanent by spreading a little glue on the wire before threading the beads, and trim the wire leaving a little extra for fixing into position at top and bottom. When the glue has set, paint or spray with a layer of gesso (a very fine plaster used by artists to prime a surface for painting). The extra wire at top and bottom can be glued into a small hole made with a pin or a sharp biological probe (always a very useful model-making tool to keep at hand), to provide a really firm fixing. A run of identical balusters, thicker and chunkier versions of staircase spindles, are best produced by casting them from a mould as described below.

CASTING TECHNIQUES

For casting objects in plaster, you must first have an object from which to make a mould. This can be a 'found' object, such as a dolls' house baluster you wish to duplicate, or it can be an object you have made yourself. Probably the simplest way to make a small object for casting is to model it in plasticine, but you could carve it from wood if this seems more appropriate. To make a successful mould, it is very important to eliminate all undercuts that will prevent the removal of the hardened casting from the mould. This can mean simplifying a complicated object, or casting it in several parts to be glued together. Place the model or object to be duplicated on a small piece of board, about 2cm (½in) bigger than the object all round. Cover the object and the exposed board with a thin layer of Vaseline, or some other kind of grease, spreading it smoothly with a small brush and carefully working it into any crevices. You are now ready to make the mould. Several types of material are available for making moulds, but for our purposes, they fall into two distinct types: silicone-based or latex-based. If the object you are casting from is hard and solid, such as a wood or plaster model, then a silicone (or alginate) modelling paste works well. It is usually sold in the form of two substances that have to be mixed together to produce a rubbery kind of plastic; this is then pressed firmly around the object, making sure it gets into every crevice, and left to set for a few minutes before removing the mould. Obviously, if you are casting a 'soft' model made from a material such as plasticine, pressing the moulding paste onto the object will seriously distort it, so in this case, a liquid-latex mould is recommended. Liquid-latex is an evil-smelling creamy material sold ready for use in plastic tubs.

Paint a layer of the latex over the object to be cast, including the surrounding base-board, and leave it to dry. This usually takes about forty minutes to an hour, after which the mould will have turned from white to a dark-yellowish colour.

The mould is not yet thick enough for use, however, so you will need to apply several more layers to make a serviceable mould. The number of layers will depend upon the size of the object to be cast, but six or seven are usually sufficient. Take care to allow time for each layer to dry before adding the next coat of latex. When the mould seems thick and solid, remove the model and wash out the mould with warm water and soap. Casting is done with a fine plaster of the kind used by denture manufacturers for making moulds for false teeth. Plaster of Paris and Polyfilla are too coarse, so buy the special finely powdered plaster for casting when you buy the material to make the mould. Rinse out the mould with water, and place

Latex mould producing capitals for model Corinthian pilasters.

in a small container, hollow side up, supported by the flanges around the sides. A matchbox-tray usually works well for small objects. When mixing plaster with water, always add the plaster to the water, not the water to the plaster. The best way to estimate how much you will need is to fill the mould with water, and tip it into a small plastic cup or an empty yogurt container. Add a very small amount of plaster, and stir thoroughly, gradually adding more plaster until it reaches the consistency of a thickish cream. If it becomes too thick, it may not run into all the tiny crevices in the mould, so it's better to err on the thin side. Pour the plaster into the wet mould, flex the mould a few times to make sure it runs into all the corners and any air-bubbles are expelled, and leave it to set. The length of time will depend upon the size of the object. If you have avoided undercuts, the object can be easily popped out of the mould, and the mould washed for re-use as many times as required. Mould-making is a lengthy process, so it is really recommended only for making multiple copies of the same object. However, once made, the mould will last indefinitely, so can be kept for future use. In this way you can gradually build up a

library of moulds for objects that frequently re-occur in your design work.

MODEL FURNITURE

Often the initial stages of model construction are rather encouraging: the main parts of the set can usually be cut out and assembled fairly speedily, and the model quickly begins to take shape. The model-maker begins to wonder if the amount of time scheduled for the model could be shortened. However, the good start is often deceptive, for by far the greatest amount of time is expended on all the tiny details that can be added only after the basic construction has been completed. Most productions, particularly those taking place in interior settings, will require some scale furniture, even if there is no attempt at a realistic 'box' set, and this inevitably takes much, much longer than the construction of the larger scenic elements. The number of pieces, size, type, period and colour of furniture all play a large part in establishing the overall style of the set, so it is important to include it in the model. The director may want to experiment by moving it around into other formations, so do not glue it into position. This has the added advantage that as the furniture pieces are completely separate, they can be rescued and carefully stored to be recycled as required. Soon you will have a useful cache of assorted pieces ready to appear in other models. The fact that most furniture pieces are very small compared to the size

Hand-made model furniture.

of the entire model, does not mean that less time and effort needs to be expended upon them. In fact, the smaller the detail, the more care should be taken in its construction and decoration.

However, there is sometimes a problem in knowing when to stop: should the model sideboard have a model bowl of fruit or a tiny vase of flowers placed on it? To an enthusiastic model-maker, who takes a delight in miniaturization there is a strong temptation to carry the amount of detail to obsessive lengths. Remember that the set model is intended to communicate the designer's intentions, not the skill of the model-maker. An example is a model bookcase – a large item often found in stage sets. Having built the bookcase, you may find it doesn't look right without some books on its shelves, and then feel that to make the books look right, some titles on the spines are needed. This should be a danger signal, for unless you are strictly in control, the grey light of early dawn will reveal a tired and frazzled designer applying tiny gold lines to the backs of model books with the aid of a magnifying glass. It impossible to lay down rigid rules here, but ideally, the amount of detail to be included in a set model should be decided by astute artistic judgement, not by an excess of enthusiasm on the part of the model-maker.

PRACTICAL EXERCISES

1. **Make a scale figure.** Get a friend to take a full-length photograph of you standing directly facing the camera, then using photo-editing software such as Adobe Photoshop or Corel PHOTO-PAINT, reduce it in size to a scale of 1:25 of your actual height (or 1:24 if working in imperial). Then print it onto card stock, cut it out, and glue a small cardboard strut to the back to make it stand up. You can now see what you would look like at the same scale as your set models.
2. **A model room.** Mount the room plan you made as a technical drawing exercise for the previous chapter (*see* page 61) onto a piece of MDF or plywood, and use it as a base for a scale model of your room. You will need to take some extra measurements for the heights of walls,

windows, doors, etc. Include all the main pieces of furniture and the larger objects in the room, but do not get obsessed with too much finicky detail. As you work, continually check the scale with the scale figure you made for the previous exercise.

3. **A model façade.** Find a picture of the façade of a classical building. There are many books available containing suitable reproductions, such as the *Vitruvius Britannicus* (reprinted by Dover Publications Inc.), or the wonderfully useful *Period Houses and their Details*, edited by Colin Amery (*see* Bibliography). Convert the drawing to a convenient scale, and construct a three-dimensional model of the façade, or part of it, including as much detail as you can manage. Build the façade on a suitable base so it can stand up, give the finished model a coat of white gesso to unify the various materials used, and you have an interesting and attractive *objet d'art* to stand on a shelf in your studio and demonstrate your model-making skill.

Inigo Jones' elevation and plan for York Stairs beside the Thames in London.

5 REPRODUCING TEXTURES AND PATTERNS

Theatre is possibly the only art form firmly rooted in fakery. Nothing is real: the Verona we see on stage in *Romeo and Juliet* is not real, neither is the Italian sunlight; Romeo is not really in love with Juliet, and they are not really dead at the end of the play. Usually they are not even Italian. In the most realistic form of staging one could possibly imagine, the audience never really believes it is in Verona. However, if everyone connected with the production has done his or her job well, even in the most stylized or minimalist production, disbelief is suspended for at least the length of the play, and we become involved, concerned, and often deeply moved by the characters and situations presented to us on the stage. Even Brecht's famous technique of deliberate alienation usually produced quite the opposite effect, and audiences were deeply affected by the characters and events presented in heavily stylized settings under plain white light. An audience wants to believe in what it sees and hears, and is willing to accept what is often quite obvious trickery on the part of the actors and designers. It may be argued that the actor searches for 'truth' in the characters he portrays, but if he does not have the technical skills to present that 'truth' to an audience in a way that can be clearly seen, heard, understood and appreciated, then all his efforts are in vain. Similarly, designers must seek out the most appropriate ways to assist the performer in the deception he is creating, not necessarily by deceiving the audience into believing that the acting space is really contained in, say, an elegant drawing room or a street in Verona, but, much more often, by presenting the appearance of materials such as rough-hewn wood, textured concrete, corroded metal, and a whole host of other materials that we may wish to use in our sets, when they are actually built from quite different, more readily accessible materials. Put crudely, as far as the theatre is concerned, the better you can fake it, the better you are at your job. Designers, however, are responsible for creating two distinct kinds of deception: not only do they deceive the audience into believing that the materials they see on stage are real, but they must also create a scale model which, on a much smaller scale, and using materials such as paper, card and wood, gives as accurate a representation as possible of the full-scale deception they are endeavouring to create on the stage.

OPPOSITE: *Detail of presentation model for Act 3 of Jacques Offenbach's operetta* La Périchole: *a prison cell in Lima.*

Breaking the Rules

Peter Brook's iconic production of *A Midsummer Night's Dream* for the Royal Shakespeare Company in 1970 was remarkable for breaking many of the well-established stage conventions of its day. The set was simply a large, three-sided box with the walls and floor painted in unbroken gloss white. Lighting consisted mostly of a wash of open white; costumes for the immortals were plain jumpsuits or gowns in startlingly bright primary colours, and the use of trapezes and spinning plates on rods was more suggestive of the circus than a production by the Royal Shakespeare Company. However, the text was spoken with noteworthy clarity, and the production, in spite of what was at that time an extremely unconventional form of staging, was a magical, deeply moving and joyous theatrical experience.

Many years ago, when being taught the craft of painting scenery, the writer was told that it is bad practice to paint an area larger than about 1m^2 in an unbroken solid colour. This, of course, is an example of a so-called 'rule' that can generally be ignored in our modern, stylized or abstract scenery.

However, there is an important element for consideration here: many of the walls in our homes are treated as large areas of unbroken colour, but if you examine them carefully, you will observe that the colour appears to vary considerably depending on the way it receives light. The walls opposite windows appear lighter than the walls that contain the windows, and light reflected from ceilings often makes the tops of walls appear lighter than the bottoms, whereas under artificial light, generally directed downwards, the ceilings and tops of walls appear darker. In fact, there is almost always a subtle gradation of colour and tone all around the room. On stage, however, all light is artificial and can hit the scenery from virtually any direction – frequently from several directions at once. Even today, when stage lighting is much more efficient than when the writer was learning to paint scenery, and has developed into a

truly creative art-form, the logical concentration on lighting performers efficiently tends to eliminate much of the natural effect of light and shade on scenery, and the skilful designer will sometimes compensate for this by suggesting it in paint with gradations of colour, breaking up large areas with subtle textures or shading. Texture carries as much significance as colour on stage. For example, a structure will give a quite different impression if finished to look like rough-hewn wood or old, crumbling plaster, than if it looks like shiny new metal or coloured plastic; scene painters reproducing the effect of materials such as marble or mahogany will not consider their work complete without a good coat of high-gloss glaze to produce a convincing sheen. Even a plain black stage floor will present a totally different effect to the audience if it has a glossy, reflective surface as opposed to a dull, matt one. Although scene painters can reproduce wood or crumbling plaster using skilful *trompe l'œil* techniques, they can produce much more realistic effects by the application of materials such as textured plasters, with sympathetic paint finishes to enhance the texture. There are, of course, times when a deliberate non-realistic finish with painted three-dimensional *trompe l'œil* effects is desirable; even sometimes pushed to caricature. The designer must decide upon the most appropriate style for each production, and this will need to be demonstrated to scale in the model by the use of similar techniques.

WOOD

There are times when the designer can use the actual materials that are to be used on stage in the model, particularly in the case of wood. However, if most woods used to build scale models were enlarged twenty-five times, they would hardly ever look like the wood used by the builders in the full sized set. The grain would be far too large, the area of each piece would probably be larger than any existing tree, and it is unlikely that the colour would be exactly what the designer had in mind. Model-makers' woods such as bass and obeche can sometimes be stained or tinted with diluted inks to

Some examples of natural woods. The top three are from trunks of growing trees.

obtain the effect desired, but far better results are usually obtained by painting the type of wood required onto a card surface, using techniques such as those described below. There seems to be a popular misconception that wood is naturally brown, and whenever there is a need to render it, we are tempted to reach first for a tube of burnt umber paint. However, on observing the actual surfaces of natural woods, it soon becomes apparent that, in reality, wood encompasses an infinite range of colours, including far more green, grey and cream than brown. The brown tones we find in the wooden furniture and fittings about our homes are usually the result of artificial stains applied by the manufacturer, so the designer should feel free to render wood in colours that are sympathetic to the overall effect desired, rather than feeling obliged to restrict them merely to various tones of brown. If necessary, the colours of wooden surfaces in stage sets can be so far removed from nature that they verge on fantasy, but still appear acceptable within the context of the overall design. Judy Juracek's indispensable reference book, *Surfaces* (*see* Bibliography) contains literally hundreds of examples. Start by deciding the direction of the grain in each piece. Because the width of a piece of wood is naturally limited by the width of the tree from which it is hewn, the grain will generally run parallel to the longest side of each piece. This becomes apparent when rendering traditional wooden doors, which are built from panels separated by 'rails' (the horizontal parts of

Hand-painted wooden surfaces.

the framework between panels) and 'styles' (the vertical parts of the framework). Start by mixing two base colours. The actual colours will depend upon the type of wood to be represented, but contrasting light and dark tones usually work best.

Merge the two colours together to some extent as you paint, streaking them in the direction of the grain. Aim for a natural-looking organic effect, and avoid a regular pattern of light and dark streaks of approximately equal widths. The grain can be suggested with a darker tone, either dragging it over the streaky surface using a 'dry-brush' technique with a flat brush, or by lightly sketching in the grain with a coloured pencil such as a water-soluble Caran d'Ache. This is a subtle effect, especially when working at a small scale, and there is a natural tendency to apply the grain far too heavily, so you may find you have to blend it into the background a little with a clean wet brush.

Irregularity is the key to reproducing a natural texture such as wood: in places the grain may be quite heavy, but in other places it can virtually disappear. Allow the paint to dry really thoroughly before you apply the varnish. The type of varnish you use and the number of coats you apply will obviously depend upon the type of finish required: highly-polished period furniture or panelling will probably require several coats of high-gloss varnish, as the first coat will sink into the surface and merely act as a sealant. Even when rendering non-shiny wooden surfaces, a coat of matt varnish is recommended, as many water-based paints have a tendency to lose their brilliance as they dry, and subtle textural effects tend to disappear. A coat of matt varnish will usually restore the look of the surface to its appearance when the paint was still wet.

STONE

The popular misconception is that stone is grey, so, logically, it is best rendered by mixing together black and white. However, as with wood, even a cursory observation of natural stone reveals a host of colours ranging through almost the entire spectrum. In fact, the colour found least in nature is the dull, mechanical grey produced by mixing black with white. The designer must first decide upon the type of stone to be represented: the cold blue-grey of granite, the warm pink of sandstone, the subtle ochres of Cotswold stone, or perhaps it is to be some kind of fantasy stone that exists solely in the designer's imagination. Whatever effect is aimed at, there will probably be some grey

Hand-painted stone slabs.

plaster or modelling paste if you wish, but if you use interior decorators' plaster, make sure that it is the type that contains adhesive, or it will flake off when dry. If you are unsure, experiment first, and if it shows a tendency to flake or crumble, add a little PVA glue to the mix. It is important to bear in mind that a cardboard surface treated with a three-dimensional texture has an even greater tendency to warp than one that is merely painted, so it will need to be adequately strengthened on the back to counteract this. When completely dry, a coat of matt varnish will serve to emphasize the texture, and enrich the colours.

METAL

The term covers a huge range of surfaces from lustrous gold to corroded iron. Some very good metallic paints are now available, but they need a

contained in the colours, but experiment by making a grey by mixing blue and brown or other colour combinations with white in various strengths, using black only to darken the tone if required. Much livelier effects can be created using this technique. As with wood, start with two contrasting colours – light and dark, or warm and cold – and scumble them together to create a blotchily textured base coat, which can subsequently be worked over with other splattered or dry-brushed colours to create the effect of natural stone. A useful tool for applying splatter effects is an old toothbrush: simply dip the tips of the bristles into the paint on your palette and run your thumb along the bristles to direct the resulting splatter as required. A latex glove is strongly recommended for this job. Water-soluble coloured pencils and water-resistant wax crayons are also useful for creating interesting textures.

You can create three-dimensional textures with

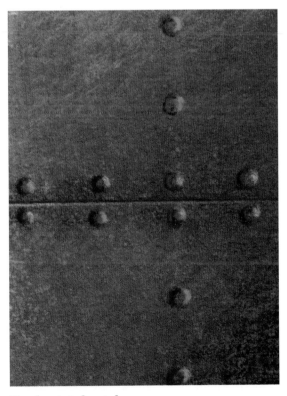

Hand-painted metal.

89

very smooth, well-prepared surface to look really metallic. Gold and silver usually work best applied over a very dark base, and sometimes the final effect can be enriched by using a base colour such as dark green for gold or bronze, dark blue or black for silver, or dark red for copper. On stage, painted metal objects are often enriched by the addition of some dark tone worked into the metallic paint in corners or around applied decorative elements, so the designer may choose to use a similar technique when painting metal parts of models. The dark colour used as a base, greatly diluted to allow the metal paint to show through, usually works well for these painted shadow effects. For iron and steel, graphite from a soft pencil can be rubbed into the painted surface, and used to highlight edges and any modelled features. However, this will need to be firmly fixed to prevent it rubbing off when handled. A light spray with the kind of fixative designed for use on charcoal drawings will usually do the job, but it must be used only in a well-ventilated space, and for big jobs, wear a disposable face mask. For a really good metallic gold finish,

gold leaf produces by far the best results. This is not as expensive as it sounds, for the term is generally used to refer to synthetic gold or 'Dutch metal'. It is sold in booklets of about 10–15cm^2 (4–6in), interleaved between pages of tissue paper. The gold leaves are extremely thin and fragile, and will very easily break apart and adhere to the fingers, so avoid touching them at all until ready for use. You will also need a special adhesive to use with the gold leaf, so buy some from the same supplier. Apply following the instructions on the bottle, but usually you will need to paint a smooth layer of the adhesive all over the area to be treated, and leave to dry for about an hour. By this time, it will still be tacky, but the adhesive will have lost its 'milky' appearance and be clear. Very, very carefully lift a piece of gold leaf from the booklet and lay it on the prepared surface. You may find a dry brush or a craft knife is a help to do this fiddly job, and never attempt to do it anywhere near an open window or an electric fan. Using a large, soft, dry watercolour brush work over the surface of the leaf, pressing it onto the surface, and carefully working it into any

Model of a portable set for a schools tour of the children's opera Isis and the Seven Scorpions *by Dean Burry, with sarcophagus finished in gold leaf.*

corners and crevices. It will almost certainly flake apart, revealing some small uncovered places, but you can easily fill these in with little pieces of leaf applied in the same manner. Don't worry about a little overlapping.

Remove any loose bits with the brush, and burnish by rubbing with a soft cloth or your finger. The small micro-fibre cloths sold for cleaning eyeglasses are ideal for this. You can apply a sealant or a coat of varnish, and the gold leaf may be 'antiqued' if desired, by working over it with a dark, diluted gouache as described above. Other metals are also available in leaf form, such as silver, brass, copper and bronze.

MARBLE

Marble comes in an infinite variety of fascinating colours and textures, so decide what type of marble is to be represented, and begin with some research. Judy Juracek's book, *Surfaces*, mentioned above, contains many photographs illustrating a remarkable range of marbles. Real marble has an organic appearance, so it is best to allow the natural flow of the paint, albeit with a little assistance, to establish the base texture. Start with

two or three colours, depending on the kind of marble you wish to represent, and mix the paint with plenty of water so it can flow and 'puddle' on the surface. Apply them quite randomly with a brush or even an eye-dropper, allowing them to mingle and flow together, with as little intervention from the brush as possible. Many marbles have obvious directional graining, often in white, running through the base colours, which gives them their distinctive appearance. This can be suggested with thicker paint, applied with a very fine sable brush after the base colours have dried.

However, a degree of randomness is still desirable, so begin by rolling the paint-laden brush casually over the surface, then picking into the resulting texture with the point of the brush to extend and refine the grain. Note that the grain in marble appears very random and constantly changes direction, making it very different in appearance from wood grain. When dry, the painted surface can be further refined if desired, by additional grain effects from sharply pointed coloured pencils. Several coats of high-gloss varnish complete the effect, enriching the texture and adding a brilliant shine.

Hand-painted marble surfaces.

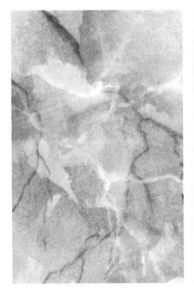 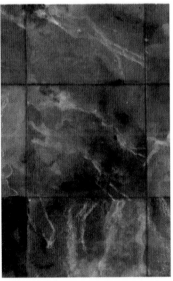

PATTERNS

In addition to textures with a natural or random appearance, stage designers frequently need to reproduce repeating patterns based upon a formalized structure, as in wallpaper, fabric or tile patterns. Real wallpapers are rarely effective on stage, even if one is lucky enough to find a paper with a suitable pattern and colour scheme, and fabrics used in the creation of period or fantasy costumes frequently need to have patterns applied to them by stencil, screen-printing or free-hand painting. As noted at the beginning of this chapter, stage reality is, somewhat oxymoronically, an artificial reality, and in the same way that actors must project their voices, expressions and emotions in an unnatural way to be effective in the theatre, so designers are usually required to create scenery and costumes that project a 'heightened' reality that is often only loosely rooted in the real world, and the patterns used for wall-coverings and fabrics need to be generally bigger, bolder, and more colourful than anyone would ever contemplate using in the real world. Period wallpapers, in particular, can create problems for set designers. Scene painters usually reproduce them on scenery by means of stencils cut from large sheets of tough, scenic stencil paper, but the designer must not only design the patterns and select the appropriate colours, but also find a way to represent them in miniature when constructing set models. Begin, as always, with research.

Many books are available containing reproductions of repeating patterns of all kinds upon which to base your design, but it is helpful to bear in mind the method of reproduction to be used in the paint-shop: many patterns will require the addition of a few free-hand strokes for the finishing touches, but a stencil will usually provide the basis of the pattern. Draw or trace off a complete 'repeat' (that part of the design that links to itself on all sides to form the pattern). Include a

A repeating pattern. Left: illustration from **The Crystal Palace Exhibition Catalogue (1851)** *published in reproduction by Dover Books. Centre: the illustration copied several times and pieced together to make a larger section of the design. Right: the design traced and simplified to make it suitable for reproduction by stencil.*

Designing a period wallpaper. Top left: the hand-drawn repeat tested for accurate registration. Top right: the design photocopied and reduced in size to be used on the set model. (The small inset rectangle shows the design when painted.) Bottom left: a small section of the completed pattern as stencilled onto the set. Bottom right: detail of the set for James Bridie's play Storm in a Teacup *on stage at the Pitlochry Festival Theatre.*

little of the adjacent repeats at top, bottom and sides, so the design can be easily 'registered' (that is, fitted precisely into its correct position in relation to the overall design). Make the scene painters happy by ensuring that the design contains no unsupported parts that will simply drop out when the stencil is cut, or are so extremely delicate that they will quickly break away in use. A little special care taken at this stage will save a lot of time and frustration later. The pattern can now be photocopied and pieced together to produce a larger section of the design suitable to be reduced in scale and used to make multiple photocopies with which to paper the set model. A little more than a single repeat of the pattern will be enlarged to full size and used to make the scene-painters' stencils. (Usually, a separate stencil is cut for each colour.) When the paper has been applied to the model, the time has come to select some sympathetic music, lay out your best sable brushes, and settle down to spend an hour or two colouring the tiny details of the pattern you have created.

Details from two set models with hand-painted wallpapers.

Miniature wallpapers for set models. Left: created digitally and printed on a desk-top printer. Right: entirely painted and air-brushed by hand.

You may feel that all this effort is somewhat pointless when it is possible to use a computer to design and print out fully coloured miniature wallpapers, or marble floor and tile patterns that can be glued straight onto the model, even scanning them in directly from coloured photographs found in reference books.

Considerations of copyright infringements apart, it is true that this can save a considerable amount of time. However, these very precise, mechanical reproduction techniques can often create a distressingly unsympathetic element in the overall appearance of a hand-built model; consequently many designers prefer to paint the entire model by hand, enjoying the freedom this gives to create variations in tone and hue within the patterned areas.

FLOOR TREATMENTS

The floor of the acting area, although usually not particularly noticed by audiences, actually plays an important part in the overall appearance of any stage set. In most theatres, a large part of the audience looks downwards towards the stage to some extent, so the floor occupies quite a large part of the average field of vision. Consequently, the kind of finish it receives should be a major consideration for the set designer. Even if it is decided that a plain black floor serves the production best, the designer still has to decide if it is to be matt or shiny, or somewhere in between. A high-gloss black floor gives a very special quality to a setting by reflecting any scenery placed upon it, so the floor of the set model will need to be given a similar gloss to demonstrate this reflectivity. In this case, it is simply a matter of applying several coats of high-gloss varnish, but other floor treatments need more detailed work. It should be hardly necessary to point out that it is much easier to paint the floor of a set model before the set pieces are actually glued into place, but it is surprisingly easy to forget this in a burst of enthusiasm to assemble all the parts to see the completed white card model. The floor of your set model will, of course, be viewed mostly from directly above as you work on it, but bear in mind that the floor of the

actual stage will be seen only from an acute angle by the audience, so repeatedly hold up your model floor to check it from the audience's point of view as you work. One very noticeable effect is the way that any lines running across the stage floor from side to side appear to be much thinner than those running from front to back of the stage. In some cases, the designer will decide to paint any horizontal lines slightly thicker to compensate for this effect. The treatment you use on the floor of a model will depend upon the treatment you intend to be used on the floor of the actual stage.

Remember that the model is intended to represent a stage set, not the real world. This means, for instance, that a stone floor that is to be painted on the flat floor of the stage in a *trompe l'œil* technique, should not be represented three-dimensionally on the model by gluing painted and textured pieces of card to the base, however effective this may look. However, the stage floor can be treated in many ways other than with flat paint techniques, and, if this is the case, it should be represented as such on the set model. An interior set may be carpeted, in which case flocked paper, available by the roll from suppliers such as Paperchase (*see* 'Useful Web Sites' at the end of this book) can be tinted to the colour required by spraying with coloured inks from a diffuser, then fitted and glued in place on the model. Single-sided terry towel can be used to represent shag-pile carpets or grass matting if this is to be used on stage. Woven patterned rugs can be created digitally, by scanning illustrations, or may be downloaded and printed out to scale, then glued to thin card or pieces of J-cloth to add a little thickness before gluing into position in the model. If the set is to have a real wood floor, this can be represented by the use of real wood on the model.

Buy very thin planks of obeche or other wood of your choice, and paint it on both sides to discourage warping, using greatly diluted inks or watercolour to stain it to the colour you need without concealing the natural grain of the wood.

Encourage the colour to streak unevenly in the direction of the grain by dipping the brush into clean water occasionally as you paint. When the paint is dry, cut the wood into the type of planks

*Model floor treatments.
Top to bottom: painted and varnished
wood floor; painted stone and
brickwork; tinted obeche wood
planks.*

required, and glue them to the floor of the model.

Edges can be slightly rounded with a fine sandpaper strip of the kind used for manicure if desired, but may need to be touched up with some stain to conceal any unpainted wood. Planked walls can, of course, be represented using a similar technique, if real wood planks are to be used in the actual set.

PRACTICAL EXERCISES

1. **Rendering textures.** Practise your techniques by rendering small examples of surfaces created from natural materials such as a planked wood floor, an inlaid marble floor, a stone wall, crumbling plaster, or riveted iron plates. Paint them on thin card to avoid wrinkling, and, when finished, trim the samples to a convenient rectangular size to be used in the following exercise.

2. **Create a portfolio of textures.** Make a collection of interesting textures. These may be photographs you have taken yourself (like the examples of natural woods on page 87), pictures clipped from colour magazines, or hand-painted textures such as those from the previous exercise. Organize your collection into convenient categories and store them in a suitable binder for future reference. This is an exercise that can never be considered complete, for the collection will grow over the years to become a valuable source of inspiration.

6   USING PERSPECTIVE

Oh, what a delightful thing is this perspective!

Paolo Uccello (1397–1475)

The architect and sculptor Filippo Brunelleschi (1377–1446), famous as the designer of the magnificent dome of Florence Cathedral, pioneered the use of linear perspective in drawings of his buildings by the use of lines that appear to recede into the picture plane by converging towards that particular point on the horizon which we now refer to as the 'vanishing point'. Based upon Brunelleschi's experiments, Leon Battista Alberti (1404–1472) in his treatise On Painting formulated geometrical rules for the use of painters. However, Alberti's system depended solely upon the use of a single vanishing point, and

it was not until later in the Renaissance that the technique of using two or more vanishing points was introduced. Many artists were fascinated by this seemingly magical ability to create the illusion of depth, particularly Uccello, whose famous response to his wife's demand that he leave his work and come to bed is quoted at the head of this chapter. Set designers only rarely need to make perspective renderings of their work, as scale models combined with technical drawings represent their intentions more accurately and in greater detail. However, we need to have some understanding of the basic rules of perspective to

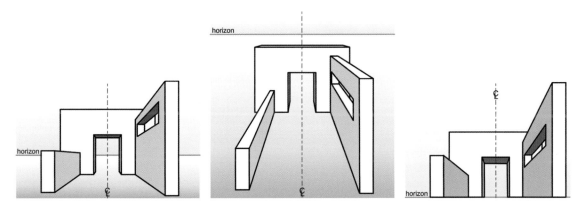

OPPOSITE: *This covered shopping and residential arcade offers a clear demonstration of single-point perspective.* ABOVE: *Eye levels. Perspective sketches with, left to right: eye level at about centre; a high eye level; eye level at floor height.*

produce even a rough sketch with confidence, and it is more or less essential on those occasions when a detailed set rendering is required.

Look at the three sketches: the left-hand sketch shows a rather basic set for a proscenium stage, as it might be seen if you were sitting somewhere near the middle of the auditorium. The sketch in the middle offers a more unusual view of the same set, looking down onto the stage. It is a view that might be seen if you were sitting very high up in the gallery of an old-fashioned theatre, or on the top of a ladder standing in the auditorium. Note that much more of the stage floor is seen in this view. The sketch on the right shows the same set as it might be seen from the front row of seats, looking towards a fairly high stage. None of the stage floor is visible from this viewpoint, as the eye is exactly level with it. The only difference in the three drawings is, of course, the apparent eye-level of the viewer. Imagine that the theatre is situated in a huge desert and the back wall of the stage has been removed so the distant horizon can be seen beyond the set. In the first instance, the horizon appears to be at about the middle of the set; in the second sketch it is way above the set; and in the third sketch it coincides with the stage floor. The horizon always appears to be at the eye-level of the viewer at whatever height he or she is situated. There are few open air theatres in desert regions, of course, and usually the horizon is hidden behind a

great many other structures, but the rule is applicable, even when you cannot see it. It is important to establish the level of the horizon, because its position controls the perspective lines, and therefore the overall appearance of the drawing. Generally speaking, a mid-level horizon line gives the best impression of how a set would appear to an audience, but sometimes a high horizon line, showing more of the stage floor, can be useful to show more clearly the relationship of objects to each other when standing on that floor.

To create the illusion of three-dimensional space, all the lines in the drawing that appear to run into the picture and away from the viewer, point towards a specific spot on the horizon. In the case of the illustrations above, this point is at the centre of the picture, precisely where the horizon line is intersected by the centre line (CL), and if you extend the lines that appear to be running into the picture, you will see that they all converge at this point. The point is referred to as the 'vanishing point' (sometimes indicated by 'vp'), and always falls on the horizon line, though not necessarily at the centre of it. Any lines running from side to side across the picture plane do not converge at all, remaining parallel to each other and the horizon line, and vertical lines remain truly vertical. Perspective lines all running towards a single vanishing point at the centre of the picture works well for objects that appear to be directly facing the

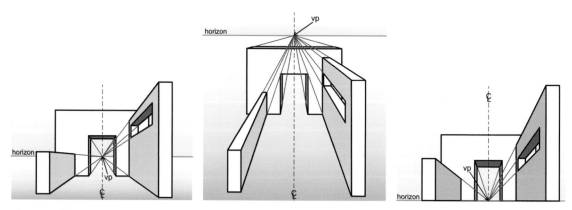

The vanishing point. Lines running into the picture-plane converge at a 'vanishing point' (vp), which always lies on the horizon line.

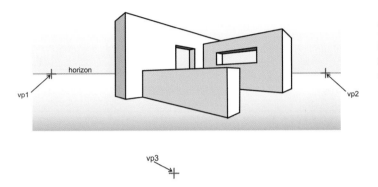

Two-point perspective. All lines running away from the viewer into the picture plane converge at either vp1 or vp2.

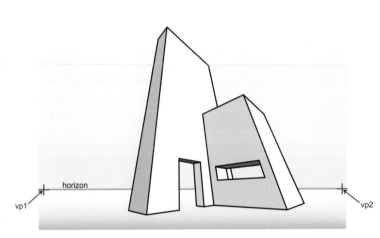

Three-point perspective. Lines running away from the viewer into the picture plane converge at either vp1 or vp2, and 'vertical' lines converge at vp3.

viewer, but for objects set at an angle to the picture plane, two vanishing points are required, both of which are still set at some point on the horizon line. In the following sketch, the set appears to have been turned through approximately 45°, and any lines running obliquely away from the viewer towards the left converge at vanishing point 'vp1', while those running obliquely towards the right converge at 'vp2'. As before, all vertical lines are parallel to the picture plane and remain truly vertical.

It is also possible to create a three-point perspective rendering, as in the illustration above. Logically, any lines leading away from the viewer in any direction should converge towards a vanishing point, and strictly speaking, this includes those leading away in a vertical direction. However, in most subjects that stage designers need to draw these lines are usually so short that the convergence is hardly apparent, and the third vanishing point may be safely ignored, unless rendering extremely tall subjects such as

Painted backdrop for Mother Goose *at* Bristol Old Vic.

skyscrapers, when a very high, third vanishing point might be appropriate. A third vanishing point can sometimes be useful to suggest monumental subjects, or a very low viewpoint as seen in the cloth design for *Mother Goose* above, where a vanishing point set very high above the top of the picture is used to trick the viewer into believing he is looking up into the clouds.

The centre of a rectangle may be defined as the place where its diagonals intersect, and this applies even when the rectangle is drawn in perspective. The horizontal centre line may, of course, be established by simply connecting the centre points of the two vertical sides, but the vertical centre line cannot be established by a similar measurement as the perspective effect requires that the half-rectangle further from the viewer must be drawn slightly smaller than the one nearer to the viewer to create the correct perspective effect. However, drawing the vertical line at the intersection of the

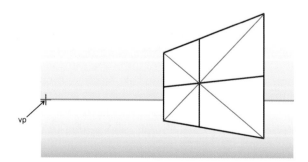

Finding the centre of a rectangular plane in perspective.

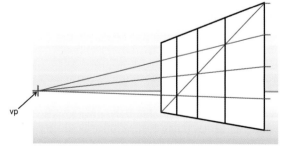

Dividing a perspective plane into equal vertical sections.

diagonals is a simple method of establishing the apparent centre line. Using a diagonal line in a similar way, the perspective plane may divided into any number of apparently equal vertical sections: simply divide one of the vertical sides of the plane into the number of equal divisions required (only four, in the illustration opposite); then draw construction lines to the vanishing point from these measured points. The intersections of the perspective lines with the diagonal are where the vertical divisions need to be drawn to maintain the correct perspective. Note that only one of the diagonals is required. This trick can be used for constructing a wide variety of objects in perspective renderings, such as glazing bars in a window or a row of equally spaced poles receding into the distance.

CONSTRUCTING A PERSPECTIVE RENDERING FROM A STAGE PLAN

There are several methods you can use to construct an accurate perspective drawing of a stage set based upon its plan, one of which is described in *The Handbook of Set Design*, published by The Crowood Press (*see* Bibliography). This method is reprinted as an Appendix at the end of this book. A word of caution: accurate perspective renderings are produced by the application of mathematical rules, and those outlined above are merely the basics. It can be reassuring to discover that a set of rules exists to create a picture, and that all we need to do is apply them correctly for an accurate rendering to be the result. However, there is an inherent danger here, for the resulting image, though geometrically correct, can often turn out to be one of unattractive sterility. Perhaps the expert Persian carpet weavers, who left deliberate errors in their work as a witness to their humanity, had the right idea. In order to achieve mathematical perfection we have to sacrifice spontaneity, and with it we lose a considerable amount of artistic flair. There is a perpetual conflict between the artist and the scientist, but as stage designers we need to discover ways to reconcile the qualities of both. The rules of perspective constitute part of a language of graphical representation, and just as we have to learn some grammatical rules before we can speak a foreign language, we need to learn and practise the basic rules of rendering perspective images, so that we can use them when needed. However, as with language, when we are truly proficient the rules become intuitive, and do not need to be carefully calculated every time we wish to communicate an idea. In most instances, lively and spontaneous sketches of a designer's concepts are preferable to drawings that look geometrically accurate but are ultimately lifeless, so the creative designer will need to apply some artistic judgement to find a happy balance.

USING 'FALSE' PERSPECTIVE

We often hear the term 'false perspective' used in relation to set design. This is hardly surprising when we recall that, as pointed out at the start of the previous chapter, a great many aspects of almost any theatrical presentation are fundamentally 'false', and perspective tricks can sometimes be useful when designing sets, particularly on a conventional proscenium stage.

A plan of the stage and auditorium will often reveal that sightlines from the end seats of the front row, restricted by the sides of the proscenium, converge as they approach the back of the stage, and if extended, would eventually intersect at some distance beyond the rear wall, rather like perspective lines meeting at a central vanishing point. The preferred part of the acting area obviously lies between these sightlines, from about the centre to the front of the stage, where performers are brought into closest possible contact with, and can be clearly seen by, every member of the audience. However, the problematic areas of the stage near the back and sides (upstage left and upstage right) can be eliminated completely by placing the physical boundaries of the set in positions that prevent their use. Performers can be brought closer to the audience by setting the upstage limit of the set as close to the

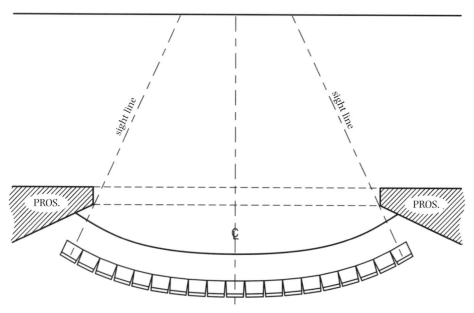

sight line

sight line

PROS.

PROS.

₵

Stage plan showing converging sightlines.

audience as practicality permits, and by sloping the sides inwards towards each other as they approach the back of the stage. This technique is most frequently employed to bring the side walls of interior settings further into the audience's sightlines, but can be applied to almost any type of setting if required. By extending the lines of the converging sides of the set until they meet beyond the back wall, a 'false' vanishing point is found that can be used to create perspective effects in the same way as a 'true' vanishing point in a conventional perspective rendering. It is not necessary for the perspective lines to be set along the sightlines, for this would probably produce an extreme, rather obvious false perspective effect; however, done with subtlety, the effect can be hardly noticeable. On the other hand, it can also be used to create a deliberately obvious distortion if this is desired. The stage plan reproduced below shows an example of this technique in use.

The perspective effect can be enhanced by using the created 'false' vanishing point in the design of other set elements, particularly those running from the front of the stage towards the back, as demonstrated in the illustration below. Logically, of course, when creating a set in a false perspective, the stage floor should slope upwards towards the back of the stage, as indeed, was the case in many theatres of earlier periods, when painted 'perspective' scenery was the norm (hence the terms 'upstage' and 'downstage', still in use today). However, almost all our stage floors are now flat, and even if we were to design a sloping floor for a specific show, it would cause severe problems with elements such as moveable furniture and practical doors, which were not important when scenery consisted solely of painted backcloths and wings. The solution is to employ another false perspective trick: if the horizon, and therefore the vanishing point, is set at a height somewhere just above the actors' heads (level with the tops of doors is usually a convenient height) and all perspective effects are confined to above this level, with everything beneath it left

OPPOSITE: *Stage plan in false perspective, bringing important elements within sightlines and adding apparent depth to a comparatively shallow set.*

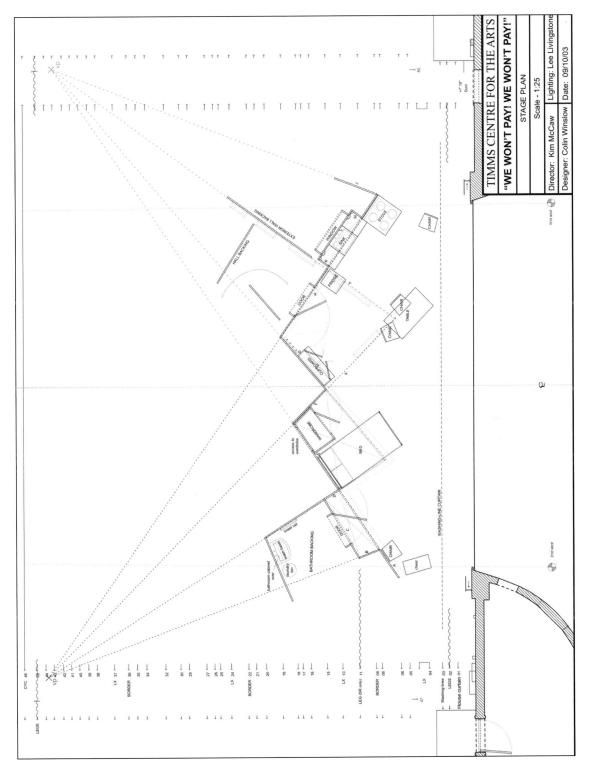

TIMMS CENTRE FOR THE ARTS		
"WE WON'T PAY! WE WON'T PAY!"		
STAGE PLAN		
Scale - 1:25	Lighting: Lee Livingstone	
Director: Kim McCaw		
Designer: Colin Winslow	Date: 09/10/03	

unaffected, then a sloping floor becomes irrelevant – doors can be truly rectangular, furniture needs no adjustment, and most of the problems created by the use of a false perspective are eliminated. The effect can work surprisingly well if carefully calculated, even for those audience members sitting near the sides of the auditorium. However, the technique is based upon theatrical trickery, and many designers will prefer to use a less 'stagey' approach, seeking alternative solutions to the eternal problem of converging sightlines.

AERIAL PERSPECTIVE

Another technique used to create an illusion of depth in a picture is to make the colours of background objects less intense than those in the foreground. This effect, often referred to as 'aerial perspective' or 'tonal recession', is most apparent in the pale blue-grey colour of distant hills, but can also be observed to a much lesser extent in objects much closer to the viewer. Although hardly relevant in creating perspective renderings of stage sets, where the actual depth cannot be more than the depth of a stage, it is a device that can be effectively exploited when designing pictorial scenery in the form of painted cloths for shows such as traditional pantomimes or musical revivals.

PRACTICAL EXERCISES

1. **Perspective rendering of a room**. Make a reasonably detailed perspective rendering of your room, including the main pieces of furniture, based upon the plan you made in Chapter 4, Exercise 1, and using a technique similar to the one described in the Appendix on page 163. To do this you will need to imagine one of the walls removed, and treat the sides of the imaginary opening as a proscenium arch, against which you can take vertical measurements.

2. **Perspective rendering of a set**. Construct a full colour perspective rendering of a stage set you have designed using estimated vanishing points as you feel appropriate.

3. **Observe aerial perspective**. Take a piece of clean black paper or card to the window, or some place where you can see for quite a long way. What is the blackest object you can find in the view before you? Close one eye, and hold up the black card next to the object you have selected. How does the blackness of the object compare with the blackness of the card? Hold the black card against black objects near to you, and then against black objects much further away. Note how black, and indeed, all colours, become less intense when they are some distance away from you, and the further away they are, the less intense they appear to be.

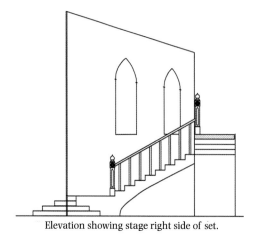

Elevation showing stage right side of set.

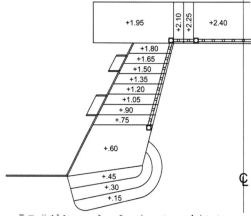

Detail of stage plan showing stage right steps.

Semi-permanent set in false perspective for NUOVA opera, with details from plan and working drawing on page 106, showing the stairs to be actually narrower at the back than the front.

Design for Jack and the Beanstalk *at Bristol Old Vic, using tricks of both linear and atmospheric perspective to create the illusion of distance on a flat, painted front-cloth.*

7 COSTUME DESIGNS

Dost thou know who ... Gave thee clothing of delight?

William Blake (1757–1827)

Costume designs are, perhaps, that part of a designer's output most easily appreciated by the layman. Technical drawings require a little effort and some skill to interpret, but a costume design can be appreciated, even if the viewer lacks any understanding of the construction process. A set model demands some appreciation of scale, which is why designers often include a scale figure in the model, but as costume renderings are inevitably based upon the human figure, the scale is intrinsic to the design. A well-rendered costume design is a desirable and attractive object in its own right, and designers often find them to be readily marketable after they have served the purpose for which they were created. Actors will frequently ask if they can buy the design for a costume they have worn in a successful production (never if the show is a flop), and although you may feel flattered by this request, it is probably a bad idea to offer it as a gift. The news will quickly get around, and you will be bombarded with similar requests from the rest of the cast, leaving you with nothing to add to your portfolio, and diminishing the value of your work.

If you decide to part with your costume designs, you will not be considered parsimonious if you set a reasonable price on them, and don't forget to keep a coloured copy for your portfolio. However, never lose sight of the primary purpose of a costume design, which, as with any other piece of work you produce, is communication. The end product is the costume seen by the audience on stage, and the design, however attractive it may be, is merely a means to attain this. It is an important intermediate step, not the final one, nor necessarily the only one.

Sometimes, particularly in a modem dress production, when costumes are to be bought or pulled from stock, a list of costume requirements can prove more useful than detailed renderings. In such a case, the precise cut of a blouse's collar, or the exact colour of a tie are hardly relevant, and the costume design can become more of a character study showing the type of costume required, rather than something that is intended to be interpreted literally. On other occasions, the designer expects the costume to be constructed from scratch, following the design as accurately as possible, but even here, the wise designer will be flexible enough to consider any technical improvements that may be suggested by specialist costume makers, or changes to accommodate a particular performer's requirements, or simply

OPPOSITE: *A designer's portfolio inevitably contains far more costume designs than set designs, at a ratio of approximately ten costume designs to one set design.*

those dictated by budgetary restrictions; provided, of course, that they can be incorporated without compromising the overall design. It is very easy for a designer with some artistic flair to fall into the trap of becoming obsessed with the creation of an attractive work of art, and forget that the prime purpose of any costume design is to communicate ideas with as much clarity as possible. As with set designs, the designer's concepts will be circulated to a diverse group of people, including wardrobe technicians, performers, set and lighting designers, the director, and often to specialists such as wig-makers, make-up artists, milliners, armourers and the like. If he or she can also manage to produce an attractive art-work at the same time, then this becomes a major bonus, but an attractive work of art that fails in its prime task of communication has little practical use as a costume design. For this reason, some designers like to produce two versions of their designs: one for display, and another as a practical working design. The 'working' version will probably be a drawing without colour to show detail more clearly, such as the one illustrated on page 25. This is a good solution, but obviously involves twice the amount of work at a very busy stage in the design process, so should be contemplated only if the designer has a particular facility for this type of work. Similarly, a designer will sometimes produce costume designs specifically for sale or display after a production has opened.

Unfortunately, these usually lack the spontaneity of the original, also all the additional notations, the fabric samples, and little side sketches that a design tends to accumulate through the production process which, far from detracting, add an additional layer of interest to the sheet.

BEGINNING THE DESIGN PROCESS

Most of us feel inhibited when faced by a clean white sheet of paper upon which we hope to produce an artistic design. There is a natural reluctance to make the first mark, for we have a nagging suspicion that what we are about to create

on the page will never live up to the vision we have in our head, so the route lies inevitably downhill from the first mark on. It is at this stage that we begin to consider delaying tactics, such as applying a coloured wash to each page to serve as a background, or suddenly realizing there is an urgent need for further research ('I've no idea what kind of gloves she should wear!'), or deciding that a sepia pencil is really essential, necessitating a trip to the art store. Lacking a scientific name for this very common syndrome, I am indebted to Professor Alex Hawkins for his suggestion of 'leukophobia', meaning 'fear of white'. The method of working outlined below attempts to overcome this. Most theatre-related design work begins with a thorough study of the script. Read it several times, and as you read, make notes of anything you feel is relevant to costume, period (even if you plan to change or modernize it), geographical location, time of year, time of day, indication of character, and, of course, any lines that refer directly to what an actor is wearing. For instance, Lady Bracknell's comment in Act 3 of *The Importance of Being Earnest*: '[Chins] are worn very high just at present ...' gives a strong indication of the kind of neckline on her costume. Make notes of any physical requirements such as pockets or handbags. Watch out for necessary costume changes, and particularly any quick changes, which might mean designing and constructing a costume specially to accomplish this. Start sketching as soon as possible. Spontaneous rough sketches alongside your notes are often more useful than words, and can sometimes form the basis of a final design.

Unfortunately, the costume designer usually has to start work long before the rehearsal period begins, and often even before the show has been cast. This can sometimes cause serious problems, such as when it is discovered that the elegant pink sheath dress you have designed for the young heroine is actually to be worn by a short, somewhat overweight actress who is, in reality, twenty years older than the character she is portraying. On occasions such as this, the designer must be ready to make rapid adjustments, or even a swift total re-design. The wardrobe team will take

Page from a reprint of Harper's Bazar *of 1898 published by Dover Books (see Bibliography).*

measurements and sometimes full-length photographs of the performers as soon as they are available, so make sure you are given copies of these. However, they are no substitute for meeting the performer in person. If you have the opportunity, spend some time talking individually with the actors who are to wear the costumes you are designing. An actor may have a fairly clear image of the character in mind, and, although you don't have to accept this unreservedly, it can be helpful to find out what it is, and how it compares with your own ideas. If you find there is a conflict, don't ignore the possibility that the actor's vision may be more appropriate than your own, and be willing to modify. After a conversation such as this, the actor should feel confident that you are both working towards the same end, and will be willing to trust your artistic judgement. A good designer always works in close collaboration with the show's director. As soon as you are familiar with the script, arrange a meeting with the director and listen carefully to any ideas he or she may have.

Work through your notes and show any rough sketches you have made. After this meeting, you can begin work on more detailed sketches which, if all goes well, will form the basis of your final designs. Most directors will not object to designers attending rehearsals, and this can be particularly useful for a costume designer. You may find that actors have been asked to perform actions that are difficult or even quite impossible in the costumes you have designed, or the actress who is to wear your strapless, white chiffon evening dress is required to spend some time rolling about on the stage floor, or that the director expects the actor you have dressed in tight jeans and a T-shirt to conceal a gun in his pocket. This kind of problem can be overcome by sensible discussions at an early stage, but becomes a much more serious issue when not recognized until the dress rehearsal.

RESEARCH

You cannot be expected to have a detailed knowledge of every style of clothing from every period of history, so some research will inevitably be required, even if the period is the present day. A great many books have been published on costume of every period, but beware that many of these books concentrate on high fashion rather than the clothing that was actually worn every day by ordinary people. This is particularly true of fashion magazines: if you were to buy the current issue of a magazine such as Vogue from your local newsagent, you would find a great many photographs showing what is now considered to be fashionable, but as you walk home, you would find that no one you encounter along the way is wearing anything like the models in the fashion magazine. Indeed, you would probably find that most people are wearing clothes they have owned for several years. So you would be ill-advised to use your fashion magazine as reference for contemporary clothing unless you are designing something like a stage version of The Devil Wears Prada. Far more useful reference material for everyday clothing will be found in pictures from

Harper's Bazar

Harper's Bazar (later known as *Harper's Bazaar*) provides a valuable source of reference material for fashionable women's clothing from the late-nineteenth century to the present day. It was first published in 1867, and was the first American magazine entirely devoted to fashion. It was originally a weekly magazine, but early in the twentieth century it changed to monthly publication and soon developed a worldwide circulation. Over the years it has published the work of all the leading fashion designers, writers, illustrators and photographers of the day, including artists such as Erté (Romain de Tirtoff, 1892–1990), Andy Warhol (1928–1987) and photographers such as Diane Arbus (1923–1971) and Richard Avedon (1923–2004). The Hearst Corporation bought the magazine in 1912, and still runs it in America. In Britain, it merged with *Queen* magazine in 1970 to form *Harpers and Queen*, focusing on the lives of the British aristocracy and socialites; however, it has recently re-titled itself again as *Harper's Bazaar* and is now much more diverse in its content, but still constitutes a good source of reference material for contemporary women's high-fashion.

newspapers and news magazines of the period. Some department store catalogues of previous eras are now available in reprint, and these can be a wonderful source of information about what people actually wore in their daily lives, even down to their underwear and night clothes.

PERIOD COSTUMES

Although many historical plays are performed in modern dress or 'period-less' costumes, it is almost inevitable that at some stage every costume designer will find himself working on a production in which clothes of a specific period seem most appropriate, and some detailed historical research becomes necessary. This kind of research involves a lot more effort than merely copying the pictures from a book on period costume. The designer needs to learn something of the historical events surrounding the period under consideration in order fully to appreciate the reasons for changes in style. For instance, women's dress in Britain during the early 1940s was a direct result of the Second World War, when not only were materials in very short supply and strictly rationed by the Government, but women were undertaking jobs such as lorry driving or factory work that had previously been undertaken solely by men. Consequently, women's clothes became very practical: skirts were shorter with fewer gathers; trousers were worn; shoulders were padded; and headscarves became a significant fashion item.

Most of the traditional adjuncts of femininity were put aside until after the war, when (if they were lucky) husbands and boyfriends returned home, domesticity was reasserted, and women's clothes quickly reverted to much more feminine styles.

New fashions never appear spontaneously, but always develop from an earlier style, even if they are sometimes the result of a total rejection of what went before, as with the fashions in France directly following the French Revolution. The revolution resulted in the total overthrow not only of the aristocracy, but also of the extremely elaborate clothes they wore. A desire for a new simplicity in dress led to updated versions of the clothes of ancient Greece, and fashionable women were seen in thin, loose muslin dresses that looked wonderful on slim girls, but were disastrous on elderly matrons. Consequently it was not very long before corsets became fashionable again, and skirts grew wider with gathers at the waist, supported by voluminous petticoats. In about 1850, in order to reach even greater skirt-widths, the crinoline was devised, consisting of hoops of cane or steel worn beneath the dress, suspended on tapes or cords from the waist. By the middle of the 1860s, skirts attained such absurdly inconvenient and impractical widths that the hoops were abandoned, and the extra fabric was bunched up out of the way at the back and decorated with ribbons and lace. Before long, this style was formalized by the introduction of half-hoops worn under the skirt at the back and known as the

| 1800 | 1815 | 1830 | 1845 | 1860 | 1875 |

The changing shape of fashionable women from the French Revolution to the advent of the bustle.

'bustle'. Thus, a study of the time line reveals a perfectly logical development from the thin muslin dresses of 1800 to the rigid formality of fashionable women's clothing in 1880.

By tracing the line of development in this way, a particular period can be better appreciated than by concentrating solely on the year in question, and the designer is enabled to invent period clothing appropriate to a specific character, rather than slavishly copying illustrations from costume books.

However, an ability merely to reproduce historically accurate clothes is not enough, unless you are designing a display for a historical museum. To portray stage character effectively through costume it is often necessary to bend the rules of period fashion to emphasize some particular personality trait, always providing, of course, that it can be done without committing obvious and obtrusive anachronisms.

It has already been pointed out that in any period, few people dress in the very latest fashion. This can sometimes be turned to good use by the costume designer, as in the costumes illustrated below for a production of the popular 1920s farce *Rookery Nook*. The first costume on the left is for a fashionable, but overly suspicious, cheated wife. The next is for a pretty and flirtatious girl who has a tendency to lose her clothes at inopportune moments. The character on the right is a sour-tempered old grandmother, who was deliberately costumed in the style of about fifteen years earlier, thus greatly assisting the comparatively young actress in her characterization. As much of the humour in this production was generated by a strong emphasis upon the period, an attempt was made to capture this in the designs by adopting a rendering style reminiscent of cartoons of the period.

Three costumes for Ben Travers' farce Rookery Nook *at the Pitlochry Festival Theatre in Scotland.*

HAIRSTYLES, WIGS AND OTHER ACCESSORIES

In addition to the clothing, a costume design should also include details of such things as hats, handbags, jewellery, hairstyles and sometimes even make-up. Hairstyles are particularly important with period costumes, which can never look really effective without the correct style of hair. Unfortunately, wigs are very expensive to hire, and cheap synthetic wigs rarely look convincing, so it is always best to avoid them unless they are really necessary. The cheap wigs made

Costume design for the boy king Ptolemy in Bernard Shaw's play Caesar and Cleopatra *in Rotterdam, showing detail of footwear, make-up, hair, mouse-cage and jewellery, including a jewelled collar and chain to be worn by the mouse.*

from synthetic hair available from popular department stores have bulky nylon hair and unsubtle hair-lines, making them very difficult to style. The sort of wigs available for hire from theatrical wig makers or good costume firms are usually made of real hair, fitted and styled individually to each performer. This means that you may be asked to produce a wig drawing. You will not be expected to indicate the precise position of every wave and curl, but you should show the direction of the hair, whether is it straight or wavy, its colour and general disposition. Hairstyles really have to be judged in relation to the artiste's own head and face, so one or two fittings should be arranged so that precise adjustments can be made. If you are using a photograph or an illustration from a book as reference for a hair style, show it to the wig maker. You will not be accused of plagiarism, for it will probably look quite different when dressed to someone else's head. If an actor is to have his or her own hair specially styled for a production, it is useful to sketch the style required onto a photograph of the actor's head. A hairstyle is so individual to the wearer, that you cannot expect it to look as effective with a differently shaped head and face. If possible, discuss your designs in advance with the person who will actually be styling the performer's hair, and if working on a period show, it is great help to show photographs or other reference material illustrating other hairstyles of the same period. You may be lucky enough to be able to have jewellery or footwear specially made, in which case, you should produce detailed drawings of these also. However, as always, allow the makers, who will have a more detailed knowledge of their speciality than you, to bring their own expertise to your design.

COSTUME RENDERING TECHNIQUES

Getting the Proportions Right

The unit of measurement used when drawing the human figure is not centimetres or inches, but 'heads'. This, of course, is a variable that depends

115

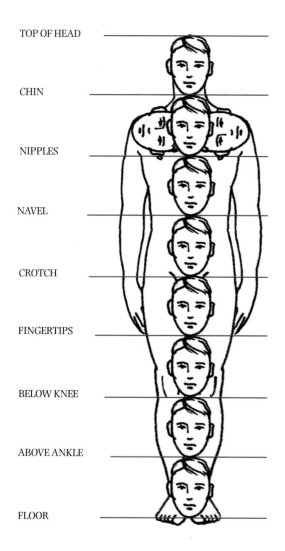

TOP OF HEAD

CHIN

NIPPLES

NAVEL

CROTCH

FINGERTIPS

BELOW KNEE

ABOVE ANKLE

FLOOR

Proportions of the human figure.

and sometimes, particularly in female fashion drawings, the figure is outrageously elongated to heights of many more heads' length to create an impression of elegance and grace. The costume design reproduced opposite, for the very elegant Dutch actress Miss Sigrid Koetse, was deliberately drawn using a height of about eight-and-a-half heads. However, as can be seen from the accompanying photograph, the actress herself demonstrates a height of at least eight-and-a-quarter heads.

The 'head' unit can also be used to estimate body width. The widest part of the male figure is across the shoulders, at about two heads. (That is, heads turned on their side, not upright.) The widest part of the female figure is usually across the hips. This dimension varies considerably, but is typically rather less than two heads wide. The vertical mid-point in both sexes is usually just above crotch height.

When drawing the human head, one of the most common errors is to set the eyes far too high. The eye-line almost always falls halfway between the chin and the top of the head, ignoring the hair. The second most common error is setting the eyes too close together. In the average face, there is a distance of about one eye's width between the eyes. It is sometimes useful to visualize an inverted

Proportions of the human face.

upon the size of the drawing you are making. A 'head', in this case, refers to the height of the figure's head from chin to crown, ignoring hair. The number of 'heads' in a standing human figure varies considerably depending upon age, sex, race and stance, but the average number is usually considered to be about seven. However, in most fashion drawings, eight heads are used to create a figure that conforms to a mythical classical ideal,

Eliza.
Act IV.
Sigrid Koetse

Design for Eliza's ball gown in Bernard Shaw's play **Pygmalion** *for Ensemble in Amsterdam.*

117

equilateral triangle with the base line connecting the outside corners of the eyes, and its apex at the centre of the lower lip. As with the body, facial characteristics show very wide variations depending upon age, sex, race etc., but it is useful initially to base costume designs on the classic proportions as outlined above, and then adjust them as required. Costume designs based upon an illogically proportioned figure will result in a finished costume that only vaguely resembles the design, and can sometimes cause serious problems for the costume maker.

Some Rendering Hints

Start, as always, with rough sketches, and discuss them with the director before you commit yourself to final designs. Describing your ideas without some kind of image in front of you is rarely a good idea, as your words may mean something totally different to the director than they do to you, and vague terms such as 'wide' or 'full' can be interpreted totally differently without some visual reference, however simple or crude. It is also a good idea to discuss your ideas with the costume makers before the designs are finalized, as their specialist knowledge can often inspire creative adjustments, and prevent technical problems at a later stage. Use the same size sheet for all the costume designs relating to a production, and don't make then too small. A3 (or ANSI B) is a good size, allowing space for explanatory notes and detail sketches around the design. Anything less than A4 (or ANSI A) can appear inconveniently cramped, and difficult to display at production meetings, for example. It's a good idea to start by lightly marking a short horizontal line 2–3cm (1in) from the top of the page to indicate the top of the figure's head, and a similar line near the bottom of the page to indicate the bottom of the feet. A horizontal mark about midway between these two will indicate crotch-level, and it should then be possible to estimate the height of the head, width of shoulders, length of arms, position of knees, etc. Mark where all these features lie, even if most of them will later be completely hidden beneath the costume. Establishing correct proportions at this stage is essential, and as you mark these crucial points, the shape of the figure will gradually begin to emerge from the page. Choose a pose that best displays the costume you are drawing. As seen in the design for Eliza Doolittle's ball gown above, where most of the emphasis is at the back, this may not always be 'full-frontal'. It can sometimes be difficult to decide how much construction detail to include in a costume design. Details such as number of buttons, buckles, pockets and pocket flaps should always be included, along with jewellery, hats or headdresses, and some indication of hairstyles. It is also useful to indicate positions of important seams, such as the waist seam (or lack of it) on a dress, or any seams that you want to be placed in some unexpected position. However, although you need to be familiar with basic cutting techniques, and carefully research any special or unusual techniques your costumes may require, you cannot be expected to have the same amount of detailed knowledge as a professional cutter. Every sheet of costume designs should clearly show the name of the character portrayed, and, in the case of multiple costumes for the same character, the number of the act and scene in which they are worn. Also include the name of the performer who is to wear the costume. The useful theatrical convention is always to use first and second names as they appear on the cast list, prefixing them with 'Mr' or 'Miss', regardless of age or marital status.

STYLE

Your personal rendering style is something that develops as you produce more and more designs. Some designers like to draw the figure in complete detail before adding colour, and others use only the sketchiest amount of drawing before starting to work in colour. Use whichever method feels best to you. Colouring a finished drawing can sometimes result in an unfortunate 'painting-by-numbers' appearance if carried out mechanically, but does have the advantage that suitable fabrics can be selected using the drawing as reference before applying colour, then painting the designs with the selected fabrics at hand, thus ensuring that the colours and patterns in the fully rendered designs match those of the finished costumes very closely.

Designs for Bertolt Brecht's musical play Happy End *for Het Groot Limburgs Toneel in Maastricht.*

(The designs for *Rookery Nook* on page 114 were done using this technique.) There is a danger that the finer details of the underlying drawing, such as seams, buttons, and applied decoration can be obscured by the application of colour, so if you decide to produce completed drawings before colouring the designs it is a good idea to scan or photocopy them while they are still in pencil. If they are on large sheets, they can be simultaneously reduced to a more convenient size for carrying around with you when shopping for fabrics or trimmings, preserving the originals in pristine condition. Sometimes you may like to adopt a rendering style that relates to the style of the production, such as the 1920s costumes on page 114, or those for Brecht's musical comedy *Happy End* reproduced above, but in doing this, care should always be taken not to jeopardize the clarity of the design.

THE BACKGROUND ISSUE

Design students and young designers sometimes feel confused when they observe that some professional costume designs are rendered against a coloured or textured background, whereas others leave the white page surrounding the figure completely untouched. Some experienced designers point out that as costumes are never seen against a pure white background on stage, it can be misleading to render them as such. Other designers will tell you that as the primary purpose of a costume design is to offer the clearest possible impression of the costume under consideration, tinted or textured backgrounds merely serve to obfuscate them. You must decide for yourself, but here are some points to be considered:

- A coloured or textured background should never be allowed to dominate the design it carries. Keep background colours subdued, and related in some way to the colours in the costume and/or the set. You may find that the water in the jar in which you have washed your brushes when painting the set model, containing a mixture of all the colours you have used, can be diluted to provide an acceptable background wash directly related to the colours of the set.

- Rendering a design in watercolour on a

previously painted or textured page can mean that you lose the advantage of using the white paper beneath the paint to produce subtle tints and highlights, and this can sometimes result in an overall lack of brilliance. It is therefore usually preferable to apply background tone around the figure as you work, rather than painting the figure on sheets you have previously prepared.

• Never be tempted to try to disguise a lack of drawing skill, or a too hastily rendered design, by the use of a heavily textured background. Experience has shown that this does not work.

SELECTING FABRICS

It is often argued that the choice of suitable fabrics is the most important step in the creation of a successful costume. However, the precise colour or pattern is not the sole consideration in the selection: qualities such as weight, thickness, texture, the degree of stiffness, or its ability to drape are far more significant. Feel the fabric; weigh it in your hands and observe how it behaves.

Try to judge if it will fall in the way intended. Unroll a considerable length of it to see how a large piece drapes. A tiny sample with hardly any weight cannot show this, so ignore any black looks you may get from shop assistants. Be prepared to adjust your design and adapt to the fabrics that are available if this becomes necessary. It is rarely essential to match the colours in your design exactly, and in searching for a precise colour match you can easily overlook an ideal type of fabric in a different colour that is just as suitable with a slight change in your colour-palette. In any case, the colour of a fabric is superficial, and can often be adjusted by dying or tinting, but its other qualities are inherent and impossible to change. Few designers enjoy the luxury of having the services of a buyer to hunt down fabrics and bring back samples for their approval, so you will almost certainly need to go fabric shopping yourself, accompanied by the costume supervisor who will offer good advice on your choice of fabric, work out the amounts of fabric required, and quickly let you know if you are contemplating a fabric that is too

expensive for the budget to bear. It can often be difficult to select the best fabrics without considering them in combination with other fabrics that will be seen with them, so a preparatory trip around the stores to sample fabrics is usually required before making the final selection. Shops will usually be willing to give free samples, especially if you have your folder of costume designs in your hand, indicating that there is a strong possibility of a sizeable purchase. To judge the quality of a fabric you need a piece of a reasonable size: say, at least $8cm^2$ ($3in^2$), so if you find that the only samples the assistant at the store is willing to provide are smaller than the size of a postage stamp, try asking to buy a length of 10cm of each fabric you are interested in. The amount of tedious effort involved in cutting very small amounts from a great number of heavy rolls will often result in an offer of larger free samples; even if it doesn't, it is worth laying out a small amount from your costume budget to acquire some decent fabric samples.

Shopping in a large city has obvious advantages over a small provincial town, where choice may be severely limited, and the more unusual fabrics quite unavailable, so be prepared to travel. Specialist shops such as Borovick Fabrics Ltd. in Berwick Street in central London have staff who are used to designers and their needs, are generous with their samples, and carry a huge array of fabrics that are unobtainable elsewhere. You can even request samples by email (see Useful Web Sites at the end of this book.)

HISTORICAL CHARACTERS

In designing costumes for historical plays, it is easy for the designer to become obsessed with period accuracy to the exclusion of character. In a period piece, the usual signs that help us to assess character traits – such as class, wealth, age, aestheticism, athleticism, vulgarity or refinement – may be lacking, so the designer often needs to find other ways to suggest significant character traits through the costume, sometimes by the introduction of deliberate anachronisms. A costume that is merely historically accurate is not

Two designs for Henry VIII in Jean Canolle's play Het Paard van de Koning *(The King's Mare) for Ensemble in Amsterdam.*

enough, even when portraying familiar historical characters, for we need to show them as they are portrayed by the specific production we are working on, and this may not necessarily be the way they appear in the history books. The illustration above shows two costumes for King Henry VIII, neither of which is historically accurate. The first design shows the King as he appeared early in the play, aged forty-nine and dressed deliberately to impress his new bride, Anne of Cleves, with his still youthful vitality. Later in the play we see him as a grotesquely overweight old man, hardly able to walk. The actor was concerned about wearing a large amount of uncomfortable padding for this very long role, so the change was effected mainly by the huge, fur-lined cape, worn doubled back upon itself, which added a

considerable amount of extra bulk without fitting tightly to the body, and without the need for additional padding. The very thick double collar, with extra padding inside, had the effect of shortening the actor's neck.

In Robert McLellan's play *Jamie the Saxt*, King James VI of Scotland is presented as an unconventional monarch who prefers to reject the traditional trappings of royalty in favour of raucous stag-hunts with his cronies. For this reason, the King's and his courtiers' costumes, although reasonably historically accurate in form and style, were made from the kind of thick woollen tweeds traditionally associated with the 'huntin', shootin' and fishin'' aristocracy of more recent times, instead of the silks and velvets seen in contemporary portraits. (Note the fabric sample

Bonnet with feather- not hat.

3/17/1

KING JAMES VI
- MR RON BAIN
1st costume

hat covered in pleated fabric

Satin band twisted with gold beads

gauntlet gloves decorated with braid →

Woolen doublet & breeches.
Prac. buttons on doublet
Tunic from leather.

Preferably old boots

Boots + spurs.

No braid

Design for King James VI of Scotland in Robert McLellan's play **Jamie the Saxt** *for the Scottish Theatre Company, Glasgow.*

attached to the design.) Historical reconstruction costumes are always difficult for actors to wear naturally, and directors frequently rehearse them in moves that can be almost impossible to execute when wearing the costume as designed. The designer can help by photocopying the designs, and pinning them to the rehearsal room wall for reference and, if possible, asking for rehearsal costumes (including footwear) to be pulled from stock. Call in at rehearsals as often as you can; tactfully discuss any problems you identify with the director; and, if it becomes really necessary, try to find ways to adjust your designs without jeopardizing their integrity.

FANTASY COSTUMES

The making of costumes for the theatre has only a tenuous link with conventional dressmaking at the best of times, but when it comes to fantasy plays or pantomime, the job can often seem more closely related to prop-making than dressmaking. Even the most expert dressmakers can find themselves at a loss when asked to make costumes for characters such as a 10ft-high giant, a flying demon or a pantomime cow, which is why specialists are often engaged for this kind of work. The designer needs to have detailed discussions with these specialist craftspeople at an early stage in the design process, and pay careful attention to any technical advice they have offer before finalizing the designs. The three designs reproduced here are for a production of Tolkien's *The Hobbit*, but although the characters may be recognizable by anyone familiar with the story, they are much more than mere illustrations, for the technical details of how these fantastic characters are to be represented on stage have already been worked out in discussions between the director, the costume and props makers, and the designer. The huge trolls had prop 'boots' that were actually 70cm (27½in) high platforms strapped to the actors' feet so they could stand on the top of their costume boots, thus making them over 250cm (8ft) tall. The actors' own feet were hidden beneath baggy trousers attached to the tops of the boot-platforms. Huge bags of polystyrene granules were worn beneath the costume for lightweight bellies, and the masks, reaching right over the top of the head, had animated lower jaws operated by the actors' own

Details of costume designs for a stage version of J.R.R. Tolkien's The Hobbit *by Rony Robinson and Graham Watkins at the Redgrave Theatre, Farnham. From left to right: three trolls, a spider.*

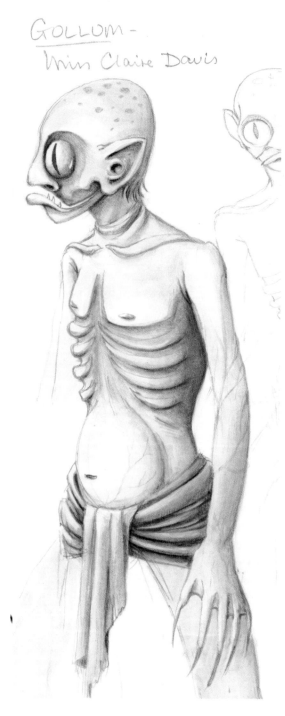

GOLLUM -
Miss Claire Davis

Gollum.

jaws, and very large eye-holes for clear visibility. The spiders' legs were provided by the actor's own legs and arms, carrying a fake spider-leg extension in each hand, and two pairs of fake legs attached to the sides of the body, all linked to each other by nylon fishing line, so that as the actor moved his arms, or reared up to threaten Bilbo, the fake legs followed the movement. Large transparent plastic hemispheres set into the masks provided good, wide-angle vision for the performers. The anatomical details of Gollum's deformed body were mostly modelled in latex onto a stretch leotard, and the whole costume painted as the design. The mask, covering the whole head, had an animated lower jaw and large, clear-plastic hemispheres for eyes. The total effect was greatly aided by the performer herself, Miss Claire Davis, an accomplished contortionist. Note that, with each of these costumes, as much consideration as possible was given to the actors who wore them. Actors playing this type of role must be prepared to suffer some discomfort, but they cannot be expected to perform adequately if they cannot see, hear, or breathe properly. Fortunately, this type of costume is usually worn only for a limited length of time, which mitigates the discomfort. On the other hand, it is sometimes not realized that a considerable amount of time is required to get into this type of costume, and this can be a serious issue if the actor is playing several roles in the production, so check this at an early stage. Sometimes the only solution is to re-cast the role.

Pantomimes are fun, but require a huge amount of work from the entire production team, so always start the design process as early as possible. Normally, the designer will start weeks, or preferably, months, before the rest of the production team. For the costume designer this presents the problem of designing costumes for performers who have not yet been cast. However, the process must not be delayed. It is not unusual for a pantomime to have anything from twenty to a hundred costumes, and the wardrobe needs to make strategic plans before the battle commences. With advance planning, costumes can be costed, fabrics bought, footwear sourced, and specialist

MOTHER GOOSE
- Mr Chris Harris
(Costume 1)

REMOVABLE BONNET WORN OVER MOB CAP.

Padded bosom + bum.

LARGE POCKET IN APRON.

Various decorative patches

RED/WHITE "HOOPED" STOCKINGS.

COLIN - 1st Costume
- Miss Gailie Morrison

Breeches to match jacket.

Fishnet tights

Traditional pantomime designs for Dame and Principal Boy in **Mother Goose** *at Bristol Old Vic.*

makers engaged long before the start of the hectic construction period, but all this depends, of course, upon a really early start by the designer. Never underestimate the cost of footwear for any kind of dance show. A pair of traditional high-heeled leather thigh boots for the actress playing Principal Boy can be enormously expensive, so check with the choreographer if tap shoes, pointe shoes or jazz boots are required. An extra set of footwear for the chorus can easily break a limited wardrobe budget, and might mean that your Principal Boy has to appear in plain 'court' shoes. Special consideration needs to be given to the

pantomime's traditional transvestite roles. It may seem odd to have to check upon the gender of the performer playing a role, but a costume for an Aladdin played by a male actor will need to be designed quite differently from a costume for a female actor, for the traditional Principal Boy in pantomime is essentially feminine, and needs to display a shapely figure and long legs. Similarly, 'Dame' roles, when played by a man, are usually essentially masculine, with little or no attempt made to conceal the fact. Costumes for personality roles, or 'audience-contact' parts such as Buttons in *Cinderella* or Idle Jack in *Dick Whittington* will

125

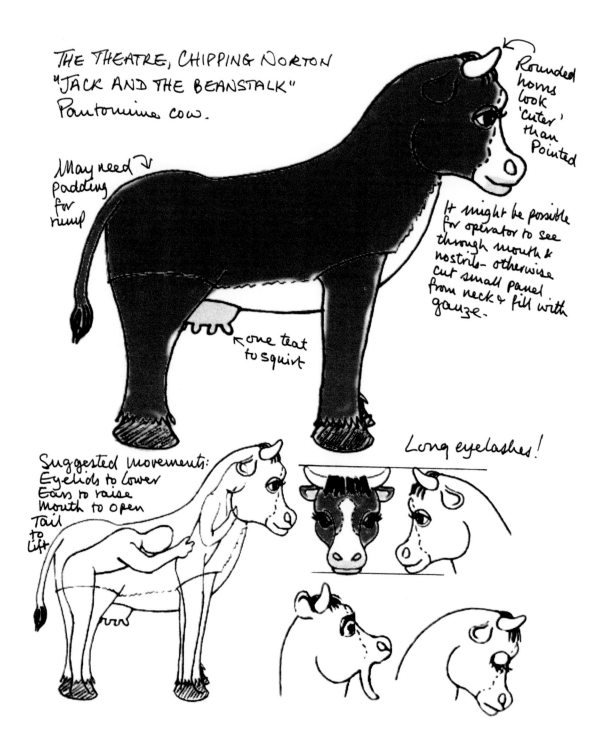

THE THEATRE, CHIPPING NORTON
"JACK AND THE BEANSTALK"
Pantomime cow.

Rounded horns look 'cuter' than Pointed

May need padding for rump

It might be possible for operator to see through mouth & nostrils - otherwise cut small panel from neck & fill with gauze.

one teat to squirt

Suggested movements:
Eyelids to lower
Ears to raise
Mouth to open
Tail to lift

Long eyelashes!

Design for a pantomime cow in Jack and the Beanstalk *at The Theatre, Chipping Norton.*

depend to a large extent upon the character of the performer, particularly if, as frequently happens, the performer is popular in some other field of entertainment. The wise designer will make a point of meeting informally with these performers to discuss costuming at the earliest possible opportunity.

Every traditional pantomime contains an animal of some kind, often referred to as 'skin-roles'. In the case of a four-legged animal such as a cow or a horse, the costume or 'skin' will probably contain two (rather unhappy) performers. It is not sufficient simply to draw a picture of a cow or a horse. The design should demonstrate how the actors are expected to fit into the costume and be enabled to see; it must also show the character of the animal concerned (cute, jolly, lugubrious or frightening), and how many 'movements' (jaw, eyes, ears, eyebrows, etc.) are to be incorporated by the maker. The more movements the costume contains, the more work is entailed, so the greater the cost. Moving eyes may look really cute, but might mean that your Principal Boy has to lose her boots again.

FLYING

In some plays, most notably in J.M. Barrie's *Peter Pan*, and often in pantomime, it is necessary for characters to 'fly', and this must be taken into account when designing the costumes. The harness worn by the performer, to which the flying lines are attached, is a fairly bulky affair, so it should be worn at all costume fittings. Check exactly where the cables are to be attached to the harness: sometimes the performer hangs from a single cable attached to a metal plate at centre back, or alternatively, from a cable at each hip. The latter type, although more restricting in some ways, prevents accidental spinning when in the air, and allows the performer to turn somersaults while flying. Wherever the cables are attached, a suitable opening in the costume is required for the cable to pass through, which should be large enough to provide easy access. Particularly important with a back attachment is a long slit, hidden in the folds of the costume, to prevent the cable from pulling the back of the costume up and away from the actor's body when in the air, giving an unfortunate hump-backed appearance.

Actor Chris Harris in the fitting room at Bristol Old Vic, patiently tolerating the fussy administrations of designer, supervisor and cutter while being fitted for his costume as Dame in Mother Goose (see design on page 125).

127

THE GREAT COSTUME PARADE HORROR

Always discourage a call for a formal costume parade. Some directors see it as essential, but it is inevitably a very stressful occasion for all concerned: the performers, making a determined but mistaken effort to show off their costumes, will usually strut about the stage holding out their arms in a totally unnatural manner; and the director, feeling that his job is to find something to criticize, will often make ineffective and tactless suggestions that can easily cause a lot of extra work for the wardrobe department to very little noticeable effect. Meanwhile, the stage crew are looking at their watches wondering why the whole thing is taking so long, the wardrobe supervisor feels his or her work is not being appreciated, and the role of the unfortunate designer is reduced to one of apologetic diplomacy between all parties. It is much more advantageous to see the costumes in action at a dress rehearsal, with the actors in make-up, performing in the set, and under the correct lighting, when their effectiveness can be better appreciated. Sit near the front, where you can see all the details, and, if possible, discuss any notes you have made with the wardrobe supervisor immediately after the rehearsal, while the actors are still available if required to make any necessary adjustments. It is always a good idea to discuss the progress of the costumes with the director during the rehearsal period and make him or her feel part of the team. Show the fabrics you have selected, and ask if he or she would like to attend any of the final costume fittings. With a bit of luck, this will exorcise the horror of a costume parade, prevent a few tears, and save the designer the (tax-deductible) expense of chocolates and flowers to placate the wardrobe department. (*See* page 156 for some notes on conducting costume fittings.)

HIRING AND BORROWING

The large hire firms such as Angels in London, which has now assimilated most of the other firms in the capital, have immense stocks of costumes to select from, and if your budget can support it, you may be able to hire some or all of the costumes for a production. It is particularly useful to be able to hire men's period suits and uniforms, which are virtually impossible to make without the services of a tailor. However, this does not rule out your contribution as a designer. The wardrobe supervisor should contact the hire firm as early as possible in the production process, and ask for copies of their measurement forms to be completed as soon as actors are available, and you should prepare detailed lists of costume requirements, and assemble some reference material and sketches to show the kind of costumes and the colour-range you have in mind. In this case, there is little point in producing very detailed designs, as even with the most comprehensive stock to select from, you are unlikely to find precisely what you have designed in the size required. It is a big help if you can discuss your requirements in advance with the fitter assigned to you; then, when you arrive for a fitting with the performer, you should find a selection of several costumes waiting for you in the fitting room. Do not expect to be able to select from the costume racks in person – usually only the fitters have access to them. You might be invited to walk along the racks with the fitter, but in this case, you are being granted a privilege. The costumier will probably be willing to undertake some alterations if necessary, and the hire fee usually covers the complete costume with hat or headdress, footwear, basic accessories, double linen (shirts and the like, which may need to be laundered during the run of the show), and the cost of laundry and cleaning when the costumes are returned. Do not ask your costume supervisor to make alterations to hired costumes. You could be fined. Many theatre companies, both amateur and professional, carry a stock of costumes from past productions, and are usually generous in allowing other companies to hire or borrow items. In this case, it is unlikely that you will be able to find everything you require, and you shouldn't expect the same kind of consideration you receive from the hire firms. You should go in person, accompanied by your wardrobe supervisor, with detailed measurements and a list of requirements, but in this case, you will probably have to pull the costumes from the racks yourself, so don't forget to take a tape-measure with you. The stock of costumes available will naturally depend upon the shows the company has mounted, and consequently may be very limited. Many costume stores are not as well organized as they should be, so be prepared for a lengthy hunt through a succession of shabby, ill-lit storage areas. Do not ask your costume supervisor to make alterations without first getting permission from the supervisor of the stock you are borrowing from, and remember that laundry and cleaning costs before the costumes are returned will be deducted from your budget.

PRACTICAL EXERCISES

1. **A modern costume**. Imagine you are a character in a play, wearing exactly what you are wearing at this moment. Produce a costume design for your character, showing sufficient detail to reconstruct the costume, and including explanatory sketches of items such as footwear, hairstyle and any accessories you happen to be wearing.

2. **Historical costumes**. Research, draw and paint two costume designs for Queen Elizabeth I of England. The first costume is for a light-hearted musical farce based upon her life, and the second is for a serious drama, suggesting that she was actually a viciously corrupt and evil monarch who sent many of her subjects to an agonizing death in order to maintain power. The costumes do not need to be historically accurate, but should be recognizable by anyone reasonably familiar with her portraits.

3. **A fantasy costume**. Produce a costume design for a fantastic character from a well-known literary work such as one of the C.S. Lewis, J.K. Rowling or J.R.R. Tolkien stories. The costume must be practical, and your design should include drawings indicating how any special trick features will work.

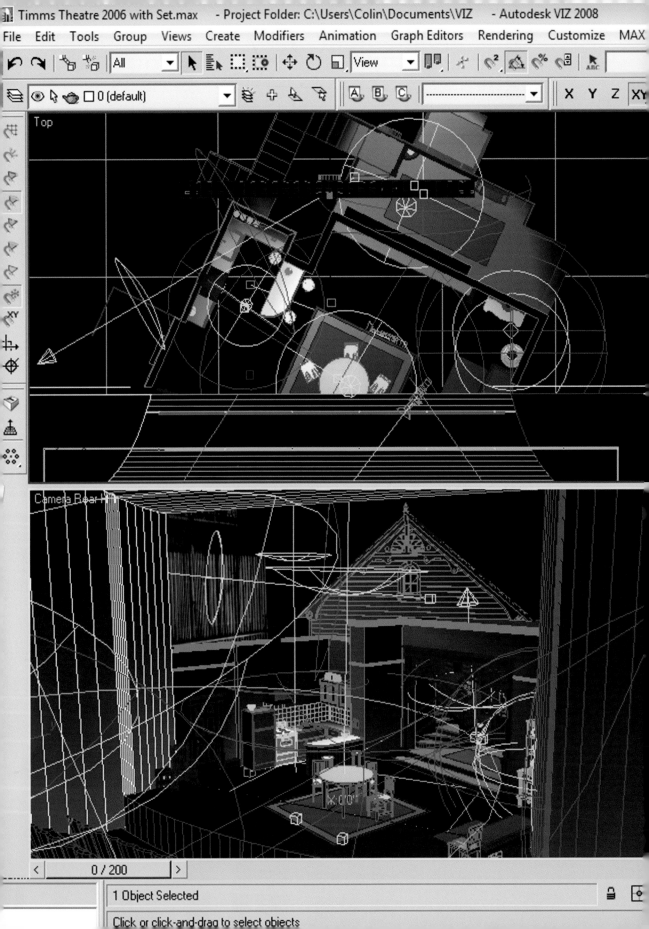

8   DIGITAL TECHNIQUES

To err is human, but to really foul things up requires a computer.

Farmers' Almanac for 1978.

There are few designers who do not appreciate the usefulness of a computer in their work, although there are still some who look upon it as a serious threat to artistic creativity, just as there are others who believe that it will shortly render all the traditional technical skills of the theatre designer redundant – and the sooner the better. The truth lies somewhere between these two extremes.

Computers have now been with us for a long time, and they are becoming more sophisticated, more intuitive and of greater importance in our design work with each year that passes. The danger is that it is so easy to delight in the 'means', to the exclusion of the 'ends'. We must bear in mind that a computer is fundamentally an extremely sophisticated pencil, for it does much of the same work, and in the hands of an artist, can be used in much the same way, but without the drudgery. However, it can never, ever replace that divine spark of creativity that guides the artist's pencil. The dictionary definition of CAD is 'Computer Aided Design'. Realistically, however, a more accurate definition might be 'Computer Aided Drawing', for, although some CAD programmes can help with documentation,

keeping track of such things as the amount of materials required, or, in the case of stage lighting, the number of luminaires, gobos and gels; drawing, in two or sometimes three dimensions, is their primary function. Perhaps the emphasis should be placed upon the word 'Aided', for as yet, no computer programme has been developed that can create original designs. Like a pencil, they are merely an 'aid' to creativity, but with familiarity and experimentation, the imaginative designer will be able to find creative ways to use the software that may not have been anticipated by the manufacturer.

COMPUTERS

Many designers prefer the portability of a laptop computer to a desktop, and as laptops now have more or less the same computing power as a desktop, this is mainly a matter of personal choice.

However, bearing in mind that as a designer you will be using your computer's graphics capabilities more than most, a large screen should be regarded as a priority, and unfortunately this considerably increases the cost, particularly of a

OPPOSITE: *Partial screen capture in VIZ by Autodesk, showing the digital set model for* Crimes of the Heart *by Beth Henley imported into a digital model of the theatre in which the production is to take place. (Digital model of The Timms Centre for the Arts in Edmonton, Canada by Mel Geary.)*

laptop. You will also need a high-powered graphics card to speed up processing time, and, as graphics files are generally much larger than text files, a large amount of memory in which to store them. If you are lucky enough to find a knowledgeable salesman at your computer store, explain what you intend to use your computer for, and ask him for his recommendations. Shop around and compare prices. The thorny issue of whether you should choose a Mac or a PC is also one of personal preference. If you are buying your first computer, bear in mind that few users ever switch, and will always recommend the machine they use themselves, insisting that the opposition is hardly worthy of consideration. When first introduced, the Mac was generally considered to be the better choice for anyone interested in computer graphics, but this is now not necessarily the case, and your decision may be influenced more by the fact that AutoCAD, accepted as the worldwide theatre industry's standard CAD software, can be run on a Mac only through a PC emulator, which makes the programme run a little less efficiently and much more slowly. However, there is little doubt that the Mac environment is more stable and secure than that of a PC, and the machines have a much sleeker and more stylish appearance. The battle rages fiercely, supported by ingenious advertising campaigns on both sides. At the time of writing (2009), latest statistics, although disputed, indicate that Macs account for only between 2 per cent and 3 per cent of the global market. Even if these statistics are greatly inaccurate, there is no doubt that there are many more users of PCs than of Macs.

ADDITIONAL HARDWARE

More and more hardware is now cordless, using a wireless connection to the computer rather than a cable. Anyone who has suffered from having to scramble around beneath a desk, trying to identify a specific cable from a mess that looks like an unsuccessful attempt at macramé, will welcome this advance. Even so, there will still be quite a lot of cables that have to be plugged into electrical

outlets, so organize them as efficiently as possible with a surge-protected multi-socket extension bar. Never permit multi-branched 'trees' of twin socket adapters to sprout from electrical sockets: they are messy, inconvenient and dangerous.

Mouse
A cordless mouse is generally preferable to one trailing a cable, but may still mean sacrificing a USB port. Try one before buying, and choose one that fits comfortably into your hand, especially if you intend to use it with your left hand. A three-button mouse with a central wheel-button is more or less essential for use with CAD software. All mice are easily customized, although many users ignore this, and accept the defaults. However, it is always worth clicking on the mouse's icon to see what adjustments are available to make your mouse a little friendlier.

Consider buying a graphics tablet. This means that you can draw on a special pad using a pressure-sensitive stylus, just as you would with a pencil, enabling the user to sketch on the computer in much the same way as on a sketchpad, with heavier pressure on the stylus producing a stronger line on the screen. Many tablets have the

A Wacom Graphire Bluetooth wireless graphics tablet and pressure-sensitive stylus.

additional advantage of being easily adaptable for left-handed users, which can be problematic when using a conventional mouse. A pressure-sensitive stylus is particularly useful for drawing or tracing costume designs and is compatible with many graphics packages such as Painter, Photoshop, or Corel PHOTO-PAINT. However, for most precision CAD packages of the kind used for technical drawings, a mouse is still the best option.

Printer

Apart from your keyboard and mouse, the item of hardware you use most frequently will be your printer. Colour printers are now available at very low cost, sometimes even cheaper than the replacement ink cartridges. Almost all of them will produce good results up to A4 (or 'letter-size'), but you may find that you are spending huge sums on ink cartridges. Laser printers are expensive by comparison, but can work out cheaper in the long run, requiring the ink to be replaced much less frequently. To produce large sheets of technical drawings, access to a plotter is necessary. These are fairly large machines, and cost far more than an individual designer's budget will usually allow, so be prepared to use a copy-bureau, unless you are fortunate to have access to one as a student, or through a company you work for. True plotters work differently from printers, by actually drawing lines with a pen instead of printing them as a series of tiny dots. However, in recent years, the quality of printers has increased to such an extent that the difference in output is hardly distinguishable. Consequently, the term 'plotter' is now often used to refer to a large-scale printer of any kind.

Scanner

Second in usefulness to a printer is a scanner to convert pictures or other printed documents to digital images. These are comparatively inexpensive, and, like a printer, will work with most graphics software packages. Make sure you buy the 'flat-bed' type, which will copy from an open book, and if you are planning to input printed text to a word processor, make sure you have an OCR option (Optical Character Recognition) that will scan a page of text and convert it to a document-style file that you can edit in a word processor, instead of just copying it as a picture.

Combination printer/scanner/copier units, which can also produce high-quality photographs on specially treated paper, have the significant advantage of taking up far less space on the desk top. (See page 135 for further notes on scanning.)

3D printer

The idea of a three-dimensional printer that will 'print' actual objects that you can pick up and handle, may still sound rather fanciful to some, but these are now a reality in commercial practice (see page 147) and are rapidly becoming smaller, cheaper, and more user-friendly with every new model that is developed. Bearing in mind that the writer was advised by a supplier, not so very many years ago, that a colour printer would never be available at a low enough price for domestic use, there is a strong possibility that by the time you are reading this, a 3D printer will be something to consider for your studio. See page 147 for further notes on using a 3D printer.

Camera

Since the advent of the first, rather clumsy and expensive digital cameras in the early 1990s, not only have they now become commonplace, but both their design and their technology have improved and prices have plummeted, rendering film – and the tedious wait for it to be developed and printed commercially – quite obsolete. The digital camera is a particularly useful piece of technology for theatre designers, for not only does it offer the ability to transmit photographs more or less instantly by email to any destination in the world, but a photograph of a scale model can work a little extra magic, by obscuring the quality of miniaturization, and enabling the image to be viewed as full-size without the imaginative leap required to do this when looking at the actual model. When buying a digital camera, bear in mind that the number of pixels the camera can display does not indicate its resolution. Resolution is popularly quantified as DPI (dots per inch), so the number of dots (or pixels) contained in an image will depend upon that image's physical size.

Buy a camera with a storage capacity as large as you can afford, and add an additional memory chip if the model allows this. A large electronic view finder can be a great help, particularly when photographing small objects such as models, and the ability to take small video sequences in .mpg or .mpeg (moving picture experts group, pronounced 'em-peg') format is also useful. Do not forget to buy a small carrying case for your camera: it is a sensitive piece of equipment and needs protection.

Portable Memory

Early home computers used floppy disks, with their useful ability to transport data files between computers, as their standard storage device. However, USB flash drives now offer many advantages over most other portable storage devices: they are lightweight, compact in shape, fast in operation, and, due to their lack of moving parts, very reliable. Consequently, the floppy disk has now been rendered obsolete. At the time of writing, storage capacities can range from 64MB to 256GB with a ten-year data retention. However, there are continual improvements in size and reduction in price. Images take up a lot of memory compared to text files, so buy one with the largest capacity you can afford. They can be slipped into a pocket or worn decoratively as a pendant around the neck. A designer can hardly live without one.

BASIC COMPUTER GRAPHICS

Computers use two basic methods to render images: bit-mapped (sometimes referred to as 'raster') and vector-based. You are probably more familiar with bit-mapped images, as this is the way a computer memorizes most detailed pictures such as photographs. It divides the image up into rows of tiny little dots, similar to the method used by books such as this one to reproduce pictures. If you look at a printed photograph under a strong magnifying glass, you will be able to see the individual dots of colour that make up the picture. The smaller the dots, the better the quality of the reproduction, so a picture's resolution is usually defined by the number of 'dots per inch' or 'dpi'. In computing terms, these dots are referred to as 'picture-elements', usually abbreviated to 'pixels'. A pixel is the smallest amount of picture information a computer can display.

The picture below shows the centre of the 'e' in 'Cousines' from the structure at stage right in the photograph on page 66, greatly enlarged to show the individual pixels. In its original format, the computer displayed this picture at 300dpi, which means that it had to perform the mammoth task of remembering the precise position and colour of every tiny dot, and although it usually employs some special compression techniques to do this, it

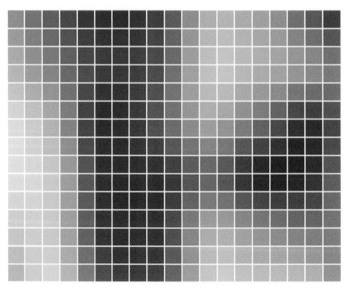

A tiny section of a digital image greatly enlarged to show individual pixels.

can still take up a very large amount of memory.

Graphics programmes will usually allow the user to determine the resolution of an image, and it is a great temptation just to select the highest resolution available, in an attempt to get the best possible image. However, this is not necessarily the case. There is little point, for example, in scanning a picture at 1200dpi, if you intend to print it out on a printer that can handle only 300dpi, and you should also bear in mind that the World Wide Web displays all pictures at only 72dpi, so attempting to display images on a web site at a higher resolution merely slows down the operation and wastes valuable web-space. On the other hand, high resolutions such as 1200dpi are really useful when scanning a very small image, such as a photographic slide, that you know will need to be considerably enlarged for display. Bit-mapped images can be enlarged only by enlarging each individual pixel, and these enlarged pixels rapidly become apparent, producing an obvious 'blocky' look to the image. The effect can have a particularly unfortunate effect on sloping lines, making them resemble flights of steps rather than smooth lines. As the rendering of very accurate lines of all kinds is an essential element in technical drawings, bit-mapping is obviously unsuitable for this type of work, so this is where vector-graphical techniques reign supreme. CAD programmes memorize images in a totally different way: instead of remembering the position of each individual pixel, the programme constructs lines, curves, and other shapes according to a series of mathematical formulae. Fortunately, you don't have to understand how to apply these formulae, for the computer is programmed to do it for you. Thus, in order to draw, for instance, a straight line, the computer asks the user to specify the start and end points of the line either by mouse-clicks or typing in co-ordinates, together with any additional information, such as thickness and colour, which may affect the appearance of the line. It will then construct the line between the two specified points in the style required. If you subsequently need to enlarge or reduce the size of the drawing, the computer will reconstruct the line between two points relative to the two original points at the new scale. Thus the resolution, or size of individual pixels does not change. A straight line is one of the simplest elements for a CAD programme to cope with, but by employing more elaborate formulae, or 'algorithms', the computer can speedily produce accurate drawings of extreme complexity with comparatively little effort on the part of the user.

Graphical Formats

Computers store images in many different formats, as indicated by the three- (or sometimes four-) letter tags typically appended to the names of data files, and separated from the name by a full-stop or point. If you don't see these letters when you view lists of data files on-screen, they have probably been hidden by default, so you will need to open the 'Computer' or 'My Computer' directory on your hard drive, and select 'Folder Options' from the 'Organize' menu near the top of the window, then select the 'View' tab and uncheck the 'Hide Extensions for Known File Types' box. Don't forget to make the change permanent by clicking on the 'Apply to Folders' button before closing the window. You should now see the three-letter file-type extension appended to all your data files. Most programmes add their own proprietary tags to file names, such as AutoCAD's .dwg extension.

However, there are also some tags (such as .jpg or .tif) that are not specific to any particular software package, and have a more or less universal application. The most common graphics format is .jpg or .jpeg (Joint Photographic Experts Group, both pronounced 'jay-peg'). This format, as its name suggests, is most frequently used for photographic images. It automatically selects the best methods to reduce the size of bit-map data files from a suite of nearly thirty compression algorithms. For example, as the computer can display a much greater range of colours than the human eye can actually detect, colours that are very close to each other can be combined with little or no noticeable deterioration in the quality of the image. When saving a picture in this format, you will usually be offered the opportunity to select the amount of compression you wish to apply. If you select a very high degree of compression, there may be a perceptible degradation in the quality of the image, so you will have to decide for yourself the best trade-off between file size and image quality, but you are usually safe up to about 30 per cent compression. This is the format most often used to display photographs on the World Wide Web, when images already reduced to 72dpi, the maximum resolution the Web can display, can be compressed to even smaller size when saving them in this format. Next to .jpg, the most popular format is .tif or .tiff (Tagged Image File Format), originally designed as a common standard for desktop scanners, but now with a more general application. Although the .tif format does not usually apply as much compression as .jpg, it has the great advantage of not causing any permanent degradation in the image. When an image is compressed in the .jpg format, some picture information is irretrievably lost in the process. This may be virtually imperceptible, but each time the image is loaded to be re-worked, and subsequently re-saved, a little more information is lost, and eventually the deterioration will begin to show, rather like repeatedly making photocopies of photocopies, instead of from the original image. Thus, .jpg is referred to as a 'lossy' format. (Note that .jpg's related video format .mpg is also 'lossy'.)

A .tif image, on the other hand, uses the LZW compression algorithm (named after its creators Lempel, Ziv and Welch), which, although not capable of the very high degree of compression the .jpg system can achieve, is a 'loss-less' or 'non-lossy' format that will retain its integrity regardless of the number of times it is saved to file. For this reason, it is good practice to save pictures in a non-lossy format such as .tif while the image is still under development, and save as a .jpg for maximum data compression only when all processing has been completed. Two other formats commonly encountered are .gif (Graphics Interchange Format) and .png (Portable Network Graphics – or unofficially, 'Png's Not Gif'). Both these formats are encountered mainly on the World Wide Web, as they offer the special advantage of permitting the designer to select a colour (usually the image's background colour) to be rendered as completely transparent, and

therefore invisible, when viewed on screen. This allows the image to be placed on a web page that has a coloured or pictorial background, so that the page's background replaces the transparent areas of the .gif or .png image. Thus, for example, an irregular-shaped logo design can be placed onto a photograph without showing a blank rectangle surrounding it. Both these formats are non-lossy.

HAND-DRAFTING V. CAD

Anyone used to hand-drafting may find their first encounter with computerized drafting somewhat perplexing. However, a familiarity with traditional drafting techniques is strongly recommended before stepping into the digital world. CAD software provides digital equivalents of the instruments used in hand-drafting, but does little to encourage a good drafting style. Indeed, it often mitigates against it, by giving the untutored draftsperson easy access to many showy tools that can often serve to obscure a design instead of clarifying it. On the other hand, a designer experienced in hand-drafting, having to learn how to use a set of new and unfamiliar digital tools and techniques, may find progress infuriatingly slow at first. However, as when learning hand-drafting, speed rapidly increases with practice.

Initially, the screen of a computer monitor seems physically far too small for drafting large sheets of technical drawings. When an A1-size drawing is reduced to the size of the average screen, much of the fine detail becomes literally illegible. The solution, of course, is to enlarge the area being worked on, and all CAD programmes provide quick and easy methods to navigate swiftly about the page and zoom in and out, often simply with a flick of the mouse's wheel-button. In hand-drafting, the size of the page is limited to whatever size will fit conveniently onto your drawing-board, but in CAD the page can be literally any size you wish, even big enough to draft the entire set at its actual size. In fact, this is precisely the way most CAD drawings are produced: drawings are made at full size and no scaling is involved until the drawing is printed (or 'plotted') onto paper. Not until then does the user need to decide what scale

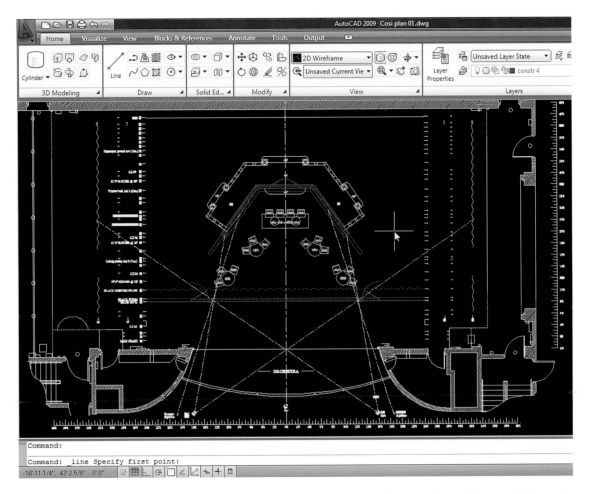

Partial AutoCAD screen capture showing stage plan in preparation for NUOVA's production of Mozart's **Così fan Tutte.**

to use for the printout. For this reason, the designer may prefer not to specify a scale in the title-box until printing, but instead, to draw clearly incremented 'scale bars' at the bottom and/or side of the sheet in whatever unit of measurement was used in the creation of the design. Designers used to hand-drafting are sometimes disconcerted to find the default background colour of the screen's workspace is black, and immediately delve into the 'Options' menu to change it to the more familiar white. However, working on a bright white screen for many hours can put a considerable strain on the eyes, and a black background not only tends to

reduce this, but makes the coloured lines, which are typically used when drafting in CAD to differentiate between different parts, much easier to identify. Drawings are usually converted to black on white by default when printing. Almost all CAD programmes incorporate the principle of 'groups' or 'layers' in some form. This is a particularly useful concept for theatre designers, as it means that selected items such as sets of flying lines, scene changes, furniture etc. may be grouped together and placed on their own layer with a specific name, colour and line-type which can be revealed or hidden on screen or when printing as desired. Thus a plan may be printed out for the lighting designer to design the hanging plot with each scene and all the lighting bars superimposed, but the director may be provided with separate plans for each scene showing all the furniture positions, but omitting the lighting information. Special attention must be paid to line-widths, for these may not appear on screen as they will appear when printed out, and lettering placed on a full-size drawing at a reasonable size for normal lettering, will almost vanish completely when the drawing is reduced in size for printing to hard copy.

Therefore, the designer must anticipate the scale at which the drawing is to be printed, and increase the lettering size on the full-size drawing so it appears at an appropriate size when printed out at a considerably reduced scale. The size of lettering to be used on the full-sized drawing can be estimated by simply multiplying the desired printed height of the letters by the ratio of the scale to be employed when printing. Thus, lettering that is to be, say, 4mm high when printed at a scale of 1:25 will need to be set at 4mm × 25 (100mm) when creating the drawing on screen. The Association of British Theatre Technicians has established CAD standards for use in theatres that includes such things as recommended layer-names, line-widths and text heights in an attempt to make files more easily transportable between venues. They can be freely downloaded from http://www.cad4theatre.org.uk/html/cad_standards.html and you are strongly advised to apply them to all your drawings.

AVOIDING MISUNDERSTANDINGS

Although CAD is now firmly established in the theatre industry, an unfamiliarity with its nature can sometimes create misunderstandings. For instance, when showing the director printouts of some tentative preliminary drawings you have made on your computer, their neat, finished appearance can easily give the impression that what you are showing are fully developed final designs, and the director may be hesitant to suggest changes. This never happens with a rough

sketch done on a paper napkin, so until a 'Convert-to-Paper-Napkin-Format' function becomes available, make sure the director appreciates that what you are showing is work still open to discussion. The most tedious, time-consuming part of hand-drafting is adding details such as dimension-lines and text notes. The fact that this is so quick and simple to do in CAD can sometimes lead the designer to fall into the trap of adding such an elaborate array of measurements and notes that the underlying drawing becomes obscured.

Add dimension-lines only where necessary, and confine them to a separate layer so that they can be eliminated from printouts if they are not needed. For example, a director may be happier with a stage plan that lacks the precise dimensions of every piece of furniture, in favour of greater clarity. The fact that digital drawings can be quickly adjusted and changes incorporated with such ease can also create problems, for small alterations in updated versions of drawings that have already been circulated may not be recognized. Therefore, unless you are very careful, you are liable to find technicians working from outdated drawings. Try to avoid this by always making sure that the version number and the new date are clearly indicated in the title-box, and that technicians know the number of the current version.

SOFTWARE

Every programme designed for the manipulation of imagery has its own particular strengths and weaknesses. Some can draft with a high degree of accuracy; some can manipulate photographic images in a variety of ways; some can build three-dimensional models that can be viewed from any angle; some can take those models and add startlingly realistic textures and lighting effects; others offer ingenious methods to animate them and store the results in a video format. The programme that can do all these things with equally efficiency has not yet been produced, so an important consideration when selecting new software must be compatibility. Before completion, a complex image will probably have passed through several different programmes, each adding its own special contribution. The list of software below is not intended to be definitive, nor is it suggested that you should buy it all, even if you could afford it, but they are all programmes that have a great deal to offer to theatre designers in one way or another, and each of them can produce files in formats that can be transported to most of the others.

ADOBE PHOTOSHOP (Usually Referred to as 'Photoshop')

This flagship product of Adobe Systems has long been the market leader for manipulating bit-map images. In fact, it has become so popular that, in spite of Adobe's best efforts to prevent it, it is now included in modem dictionaries as a verb, as in: 'This designer's publicity photograph must have been photoshopped.' In 2005, Adobe caused some confusion by renaming Photoshop 8 to Photoshop CS as a result of the rebranding of its Creative Suite. Thus, the current version at the time of writing included in Adobe Photoshop CS4, is actually the eleventh release of Adobe Photoshop.

However, this rebranding has had the happy result of Adobe issuing numerous software packages containing multiple Adobe programmes, including Photoshop, at greatly reduced prices. Photoshop is very user-friendly at the basic level, and contains a huge array of advanced features for anyone willing to invest a little time in learning how to use them. Its native file format, .psd (PhotoShop Document), is supported by most of the other graphics software packages. Photoshop is valued particularly for its ability to create and manipulate bit-mapped images, but a somewhat less popular sister programme, Adobe Illustrator, is also available for the creation and development of vector-based graphics. Photoshop CS4 contains both Photoshop and Illustrator, together with some exciting innovations particularly useful to theatre designers, such as the ability to wrap photographic images around three-dimensional digital models, or paint directly onto three-dimensional shapes.

COREL DESIGNER TECHNICAL SUITE

As the name suggests, this is a package of several graphics programmes, of which the two main ones are Corel DESIGNER and Corel PHOTO-PAINT. Corel DESIGNER is a vector-orientated programme that is an enhanced version of the old CorelDRAW.

The new version is able to import drawings from AutoCAD – a great attraction for theatre designers, although at the moment this facility is little clumsy in operation. It contains some good drafting functions, including dynamic dimensioning, and can easily produce professional-looking technical drawings. The excellent text handling functions, including a spelling and grammar check, and the ability to fit text to a predefined path are handy for producing documents such as illustrated leaflets and flyers. Files can be saved in Corel's proprietary formats, .des or .cdr, and exported to most other popular formats, including, particularly usefully, .pdf.

Corel PHOTO-PAINT is designed primarily for the manipulation of photographic images, but can also be used as a digital painting programme, with or without a graphics tablet (see page 132) to produce pictures from scratch. The programme uses a fairly standard graphical interface, which makes it easy to get to grips with its basic functions. By default, it will save files in its own

PDF

The Portable Document Format, created by Adobe Systems and identifiable by its .pdf tag, is an extremely useful way to exchange documents between computers, independent of software or operating systems. PDF documents may contain text and/or graphical material of any kind regardless of the software used to produce them. They can easily be read using Adobe Reader (formerly known as Acrobat Reader), freely available from http://get.adobe.com/reader, but users generally need to buy the Adobe Acrobat Suite to create them. However, several graphics packages, such as those available from Corel, include the option to export (or 'publish') files to PDF.

proprietary format, .cpt, but will also save or export to most other popular formats such as .jpg, .tif, .gif, .png, .bmp, .psd (Adobe Photoshop) and also .pdf. Corel PowerTRACE, also included in the Corel DESIGNER Technical Suite, is a useful programme that can trace outlines from bit-mapped images such as photographs, and convert them to vector graphics for subsequent manipulation in a CAD programme. The degree of sensitivity used when tracing the outline is easily adjusted by the user. Corel CAPTURE is a handy little application that allows you to designate a key on your keyboard as a 'hot-key', which, when pressed, will save any image that happens to be on your screen in the format of your choice. All the screen images reproduced in this chapter were captured using this programme. A particular strength of the Corel DESIGNER suite is the integration of bit-mapped with vector graphics, which means, for instance, that sheets of technical drawings, or other drawings based upon vector graphics, can also contain photographic images that can be adjusted from within the programme if necessary. A freely downloadable plug-in called Deep Exploration will even allow the user to view and import 3D models from programmes such as AutoCAD, 3ds Max and SketchUp for inclusion as 2D images.

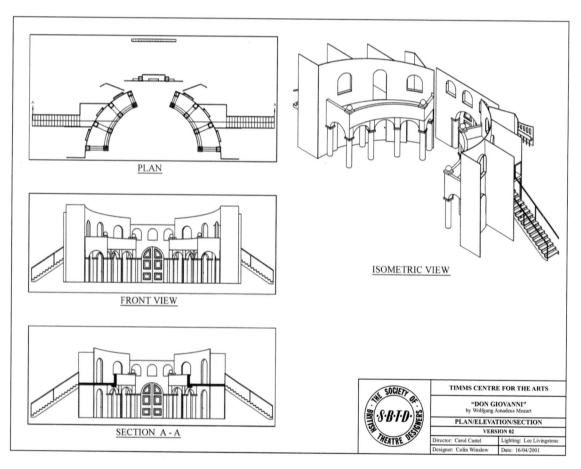

AutoCAD drawing showing plan, elevation and section produced automatically from a digital model.

AutoCAD

This is by far the most commonly used CAD system worldwide, and the recognized industry-standard software for the performing arts. In addition to a vast array of drafting tools, the more recent updates have included great improvements in tools for the creation, manipulation and rendering of 3D models. AutoCAD suffers from being a very expensive programme to purchase, but is also available in a version aimed primarily at students called AutoCAD Light (AutoCAD LT) that is a good deal cheaper, and contains most of the functions of the full programme, including the ability to create simple 3D models. Although it can display three-dimensional models that have been created with the full version, AutoCAD LT lacks the advanced solid-modelling and rendering functions needed to create photo-realistic images with user-designed textures, including transparent and reflective surfaces, and user-designed lighting with realistic shadows, such as those reproduced below.

Later versions of AutoCAD offer a 'walk-through' function that enables the designer to create video sequences showing the eye-level view of someone walking through the model along a route defined by the user. Theatre designers can make good use of this function to create videos showing the appearance of a set on stage as the

Rendering created entirely in AutoCAD of a 3D digital set model for Václav Havel's play **Largo Desolato** *at the Timms Centre for the Arts, Edmonton, Canada. Inset: close-up of the drinks tray at stage right showing reflective chrome, glass and liquid effects.*

viewer moves from one side of the auditorium to another. The main function of AutoCAD, however, is speedy and accurate drafting, and other programmes are available that cope rather better with advanced 3D modelling and rendering techniques. The primary reason for their inclusion in AutoCAD is for a slightly different purpose: imagine that you have a real-world scale model of a stage set and need to draft it. In order to do this you would need to examine its structure, take many detailed measurements, and use them to produce several sheets of technical drawings, including plan and elevation. You might even slice the model in half to draw a sectional view from one of the cut sides. However, if you have constructed a digital model, your computer already has all the information needed to produce each of these drawings, and AutoCAD has the ability to create and print out well-designed pages of automatically generated plans, elevations and sections in a fraction of the time it would take to produce all of these drawings separately, and, of course, the sheets can also include photographically realistic images showing different views of the completed set.

TurboCAD

Sometimes unfairly disparaged as merely a cut-down version of AutoCAD, TurboCAD has been developed by the IMSI software house, and, although lacking some of more refined functions of the larger programme, actually has several advantages, particularly its cost and more intuitive interface. TurboCAD is available in several versions, the most basic and inexpensive being TurboCAD Designer, which is an excellent 2D drafting programme that will save to most standard file formats. At the high end, TurboCAD Pro Platinum Edition contains most of the advanced 3D modelling functions found in the more expensive packages, and makes professional-level CAD available to the average home-user. Versions for the Mac are also available, but use a separate codebase so are not directly comparable with the original Windows versions.

Vectorworks

Originally known as MiniCAD and developed specifically for the Mac operating system, Vectorworks is now owned by Nemetschek, and, since 1996, has also been available for Windows.

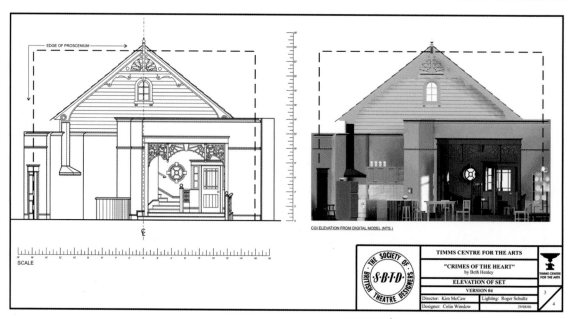

Elevation of the set for **Crimes of the Heart** *at the Timms Centre for the Arts in Edmonton, Canada, including a digitally created image of the completed set.*

Among theatre designers it has now become a serious rival for AutoCAD, especially for Mac users. Among its many advantages are its easy ability to merge 2D with 3D drafting, and its comparatively low cost. Particularly of interest to lighting designers is Vectorworks Spotlight, a programme that allows the creation of realistic three-dimensional images of stage sets as seen under user-defined stage lighting conditions, and also includes digital versions of thousands of luminaires and their accessories from all the leading manufacturers, along with accurate representation of light beams in 2D or 3D if required, and several thousand gobos. All this, combined with the ability to create automatically generated summaries and schedules makes it an extremely attractive programme. Files can be saved in formats compatible with most of the other commonly used CAD programmes. A great many software packages dedicated specifically to the production of 3D models are now available. Many of these include the ability to produce extremely impressive animations, including realistically rendered non-geometrical elements such as water, fire, smoke, and hair of the kind we see in movies such as the *Shrek* series. However, as most of this software is designed primarily for the computer games and movie industry, the construction of architectural features with the high degree of precision required by set designers is not a prime consideration, so when considering these packages, the ability to import files from dedicated drafting software such as AutoCAD becomes an important consideration.

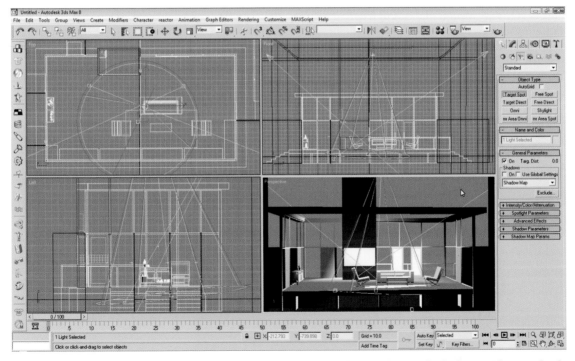

Set model for Largo Desolato *created in AutoCAD and imported into 3ds Max for lighting. The standard screen layout displays four views simultaneously: plan, front, side in 'wireframe' and, at bottom right, a solid perspective view.*

Rendering of 3D figure – created, posed and lit in Poser.

Autodesk 3ds Max (Formerly 3D Studio MAX)

This mammoth modelling, animation and rendering package contains all the functions needed to create spectacular animated 3D models, including non-geometrical organic structures, animated characters and environments, including atmospheric effects such as mist, fire and water. For stage designers it offers sophisticated lighting and rendering tools with a reasonably intuitive interface. Coming from Autodesk, the same software house that produces AutoCAD, it is an excellent programme to use for developing fine computer-generated images (CGI) from models constructed in AutoCAD. However, having been designed primarily with animation for the games industry in mind, the programme is not the best to use for the creation of precisely accurate 3D structures from scratch.

Poser (Formerly from E Frontier, Now Owned by Smith Micro Software)

This fascinating software package is dedicated to the creation, posing, animation and rendering of realistic three-dimensional human and animal figures. To theatre designers, it offers the possibility of including people in their digital set models. The figures are genuinely three-dimensional, in the sense that they can be revolved and posed in virtually any position, and will react to whatever lighting has been set in the model just as any other object. The ingenious interface is non-standard, but, as far as basic modelling and posing is concerned, is very user-friendly. The programme contains a range of stock figures and clothing, which can easily be coloured or otherwise adjusted as required, and more advanced features include user-styled hair and clothing. There is also a function to design characters with faces based upon photographs of real people, so, with a little effort, digital set models can be created containing avatars of the actual performers who are to play in them.

Rendering of the setting for NUOVA's production of Kurt Weill's opera Street Scene, showing set model created in AutoCAD, lit in 3ds Max, with figure created in Poser.

3D MODELLING SOFTWARE FOR FREE!

Unbelievable though it sounds, there are at least two excellent 3D modelling programmes that can be downloaded from the Internet at no cost whatsoever. All you have to do to get them is log on to a web site and hit the appropriate download buttons, having first temporarily disabled your computer's virus protection software to give the programme access to your hard drive.

Google SketchUp

To download it, go to http://sketchup.google.com and follow the on-screen installation instructions. SketchUp works in more or less the same way with both Windows and Mac operating systems. Apart from being totally free, SketchUp has the advantage of being by far the most user-friendly modelling software to use. Google has tried to make the interface as intuitive as possible, and you will find you can quickly get to grips with the basic functions. However, the programme also contains some surprisingly advanced features, which can be accessed with very little effort. Where SketchUp falls short is in the creation of really accurate plans on which to base the models, but drawings from CAD programmes such as AutoCAD can be imported and either extruded directly into the third dimension, or used to provide an accurate base on which to model the 3D structures. Google has created many excellent video tutorials, aimed at both beginners and more advanced users, available free at http://sketchup.google.com /training/videos.html. If you would like to take things further, Google SketchUp Pro is available for purchase at a reasonable price.

Blender

It seems extraordinary that this very sophisticated, professional-level 3D modelling and animation software is available totally free. With it, you can create almost anything you can imagine, and, even more surprising, the programme takes up a mere 9MB on your hard drive. It runs happily on almost any operating system, including Linux, and can be

The Utah Teapot

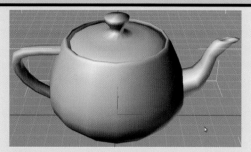

The 3ds Max version of the Utah teapot.

Users new to 3D modelling programmes such as 3ds Max are frequently surprised to find a rather nice teapot included in the programme's collection of basic geometrical shapes or 'primitive solids'. Compared with the usual cubes, spheres and pyramids, the teapot hardly seems 'primitive'.

Actually, the so-called 'Utah Teapot' has quite a distinguished history: it was first created by a computer graphics researcher named Martin Newell at the University of Utah in 1975, hence its name. It was designed as a model for testing advances in 3D graphics, and because of its irregular curves, the hole contained in the handle, the shadow it casts upon itself, and the fact that it retains its integrity without the addition of complex surface textures, it has proved to be an excellent experimental model. Some programmes, however, prefer to assert their individuality by replacing the teapot with a different test object: Blender, for example, uses a monkey's head called Suzanne, after the orang-utan in the film *Jay and Silent Bob Strike Back*.

Newell constructed his first model by digitizing his wife's teapot, and because in those days the construction of digital models meant laboriously entering a large number of complex co-ordinates 'by hand', he generously made his data available to other researchers. Newell employed rectangular rather than square pixels, so the first teapots turned out rather squat, and as they were not intended to be viewed from underneath, they had no base. The teapots used today were modified by his colleague James Blinn to correct these deficiencies. The original teapot, bought from a department store in Salt Lake City, is now on display in the Computer History Museum in Mountain View, California.

downloaded at http://www.blender.org/download /get-blender, where you will also find a users' gallery of images that will astonish you. There is also a link to the impressive *Elephants Dream* video created entirely in Blender; and some helpful tutorials. Blender contains many advanced features such as water simulation and soft-body, cloth and particle dynamics, normally found only in expensive high-end packages. Blender is constantly under development by skilled programmers worldwide, under the control of the Blender Foundation, chaired by Ton Roosendaal, the software's original author and mastermind. Blender's only drawback is its non-standard interface which makes it a tricky programme to come terms with, and (*pace* Chris Want) can hardly be described as 'user-friendly'. The learning-curve is fairly steep, and you will need to devote a considerable amount of time working through tutorials before it becomes of practical use. However, it is powerful software that will repay the effort.

LEARNING HOW TO USE THE SOFTWARE

Although software houses pay a great deal of attention to making their software as easy to use as possible, the complexity of most of the packages outlined above means that it can take some time for the user to become really proficient. The best way to learn is to attend classes, but unfortunately, as this is not possible for most of us, we have to find ways of getting to grips with it alone. Do not despair if it seems to take some time before you can produce anything really useful from a new piece of software. It probably took a good deal of time for you to use a simple pencil with fluency and proficiency, and as the facilities offered by your computer are much more elaborate than a pencil, it is logical that these skills should take some time to acquire. You will find that many books are published to accompany new releases of the all the popular software packages, many of them very thick, expensive, and claiming to be the manufacturer-approved, definitive reference

manual. However, bear in mind that these software 'bibles' are designed primarily as reference books, and although they describe all the functions of the software in considerable detail, they do not provide the best way to become familiar with its use (in much the same way as buying a dictionary is not the best way to learn to speak a language). Instead, look for tutorial books that contain a graded series of lessons with exercises to be worked through. The *... for Dummies* series does this quite effectively, if you can cope with the persistent jocular tone, but there are many others, some of which are listed in the Bibliography section at the end of this book. Whichever book you choose, remember that real progress comes from practice, not reading, so spend as much time playing and experimenting with new software as possible, and force yourself to use it in your design work, even if, initially, it tends to slow down the work rather than speeding it up. Speed will come with familiarity.

PRINTING IN 2D AND 3D

In spite of the fact that so much of our design work is computer-based, hard-copy prints that can be tucked into a folder or pinned up on a wall are still usually required. As it is unlikely that an individual designer will own a large-scale printer/plotter that can handle up to A0 size drawings, you will usually have to take data files of stage plans and technical drawings to a commercial printing bureau. First check what formats it can handle, for much time and additional expense can be saved by submitting the data in a form that requires as little work as possible on the part of the copy bureau. Your original CAD drawings were probably produced at full size, so reduce them to the scale you require for the hard copy before submitting them to the printer, and add the scale to the title-box to avoid misunderstandings. Check if your bureau will accept work by email, and let you know when the prints are ready for collection, and don't forget to tell them if you need large prints to be folded or rolled. Workshops usually prefer rolled drawings to lay out flat on a drawing-board, but the director would probably like them neatly folded to slip in a briefcase (*see* page 60). You will need to print

146

several different versions of the stage plan: stage management may appreciate a copy with all the dimensions marked as an aid to marking out the set in the rehearsal room, but as this can sometimes make the plan confusing to read, also print out an un-dimensioned copy for the director and another one to display on the wall of the rehearsal room. Copies of the stage plan and set rendering, reduced to A4 or 'letter' size, can be printed out on a desktop printer and given to actors to keep in their scripts for reference, and don't forget that the stage manager will need a small, greatly simplified and un-dimensioned version of the plan showing furniture positions to copy and paste into the prompt copy of the script for plotting actors' moves as they become established in rehearsal.

USING A 3D PRINTER

Visit http://www.zcorp.com or http://www.tech soft.co.uk for details of 3D printers and other CAD/CAM hardware. Various methods are used to create actual objects from 3D digital files but most commonly, the 3D printer lays down a very thin layer of fine plaster, about 0.1mm thick, which can be hardened by the application of a special liquid from an arm similar to one in an ordinary ink-jet printer. The computer scans the first layer of the image, and applies the hardening ink-solution to the plaster powder in those areas it recognizes as solid. The base-plate then sinks by the depth of a layer of the plaster, and a second layer of plaster-dust is laid on top of the first; the second layer of the image is scanned, and again, the appropriate areas of plaster are hardened. This process is

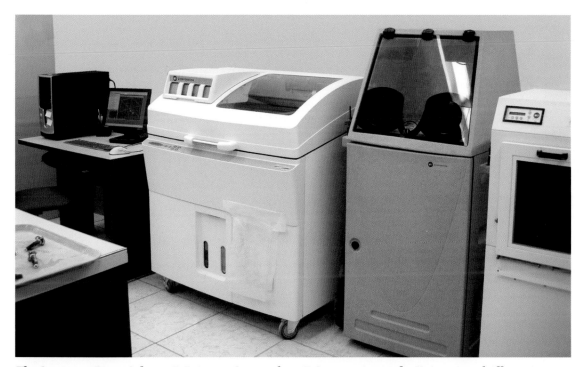

The Spectrum Z510 Colour 3D Printing System from Z Corporation at the University of Alberta in Canada. From left to right: computer with monitor showing position of the objects being printed; the printer; airbrush cabinet; waxing cabinet.

repeated until the whole object has been built up in hardened plaster. The model is then removed, and the surplus powder removed with an airbrush for recycling. The model may then be coated in wax for a smoother finish and extra strength. The Spectrum Z510 model in the photograph above prints objects in full 24-bit colour at 600dpi. There is, of course, a size limitation: the maximum size the printer illustrated can handle is 254mm × 356mm × 203mm (10in × 14in × 8in). You can see a video of it in action at http://www.ualberta.ca/CNS/3DPRINTER. Using this method, undercuts, hollow objects, or even loose objects inside other objects present no problem for the printer. Before sending files to a 3D printer, find out what file formats the printer can handle. There are various options, so select a format that your software includes in its 'Export to

...' list. Most 3D modelling programmes will export directly to .stl (Sterolithography) or .vrml (Virtual Reality Modelling Language, usually pronounced 'vermal'), which most 3D printers understand. When converting files to these formats bear in mind:

- .vrml will retain colour information, but .stl does not.
- .stl format cannot handle negative numbers, so you may need to move your on-screen model to a position beyond, above, and to the right of the 0,0,0 co-ordinate before exporting it to .stl in order for the conversion to work.
- You have probably constructed your digital model at full size, so don't forget to scale it down to the size you require before converting to a printer format. Unfortunately, the 3D printer

Screen capture from 3D printer's monitor when printing a complete set model for NUOVA's production of Mozart's Don Giovanni.

1:25 scale furniture and figures, designed in AutoCAD and Poser respectively, and printed by the Z Corp 510 3D printer. (Armchair painted by hand.)

that can print out a full-sized stage set is not yet available. You may be pleased to learn, however, that machines are now being developed that use similar technology to produce real houses for people to live in, so presumably, machines that can produce full-size, usable stage sets from digital models are not too far away.

Models produced by a 3D printer as described above are surprisingly detailed, but, especially if they contain very slender parts, such as small-scale chair-legs or banisters, can be somewhat fragile. Experimentation has shown they can be hardened by dribbling thin cyanoacrylate over them. However, as previously mentioned (*see* page 72) this active ingredient of superglue can be dangerous when mishandled. Always handle it with extreme care, and never use it without a solvent at hand. A coat of gesso after hardening will provide a good surface for painting with gouache or acrylic, and help to conceal the slightly granular surface of the unpainted model.

USING A SCANNER

Do not be tempted to scan at the highest resolution available, as this is hardly ever really necessary and will only result in huge, unmanageable files. There is little point in scanning images at extremely high resolutions if they are to be printed out at 300dpi. On the other hand, if you wish to enlarge an extremely small image by a great extent, scanning at a high resolution will produce a more detailed final image. It is not often realized that scanners can also cope quite successfully with small three-dimensional objects. This can sometimes prove useful to a designer who has photographed a set model, and passed it to the workshop for costing, before making the model furniture: the miniature furniture can be scanned by simply being laid on the scanner's platen. It is then not difficult to lift the scanned image of the furniture from its plain background, and using a programme such as Photoshop or Corel PHOTO-PAINT, superimpose it onto a photograph of the set, scale it to the correct size, move to the desired position, and merge it into

Costume design developed from a 'thumbnail' sketch on the corner of a paper napkin (inset at bottom left), scanned, enlarged, printed out, and finished by hand in gouache and coloured pencil.

photograph. Using a similar technique, photographs of items of furniture in a store, or scanned from catalogues, can also be merged into a photograph of the set model. For costume designers, there is the possibility of scanning selected fabrics, reducing them to a much smaller scale, and filling scanned costume drawings with the actual fabric patterns. If, like the writer, you find your rough, 'thumbnail' sketches, casually dashed off on a scrap of waste paper, more attractive than your carefully considered final designs, try scanning the roughs at a fairly high resolution and enlarging them to A3 size. Print them onto thin card-stock and work over them with gouache or coloured inks and pencil for the final version.

USING A WEB SITE

There are some notes about setting up a personal web site on page 157, but if you have rented some space on the World Wide Web, and attained some proficiency in creating web pages, it is a comparatively simple matter to set up small temporary web sites for the shows you are working on. To maintain privacy, these should have no links from any other sites, so that only those people who have been given the address (or URL – Uniform Resource Locator) will be able to log on to it. The site might contain the contact numbers for technical departments, cast list and costume designs, photographs of the set model, and technical drawings in both AutoCAD and .pdf formats. When the show has opened, the web site can be dismantled and the space re-claimed.

KEEPING UP TO DATE

The digital world progresses at an alarming and ever-increasing rate. By the time you are reading this, much of the software described in this chapter will have been already supplanted by newer, improved versions, which is why no version numbers have been included in the descriptions. The major software houses bring out updated versions of their popular programmes almost yearly, and quite understandably, they do their very best to persuade us to upgrade to the newest

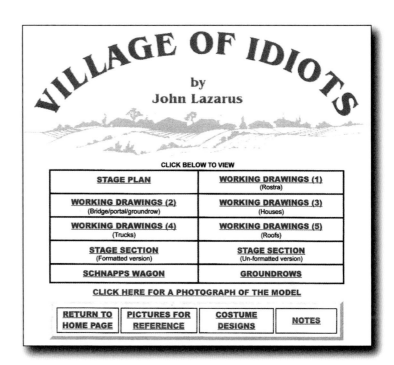

Temporary production web site for Village of Idiots *at Red Deer College, Canada.*

version. However, before upgrading, it is worthwhile checking to see exactly what you will be getting for the extra money, for although some upgrades genuinely offer major improvements, others are mostly cosmetic. The software that excited you when you bought it a couple of years ago, probably still works just as efficiently as it did when you first installed it, so unless you feel the newer version will make a genuine improvement in your productivity, as opposed to merely offering a prettier interface, you should resist the impulse to upgrade. It was pointed out at the start of this chapter that, for the designer, the computer functions merely as an elaborate substitute for a pencil, so we should not overlook the fact that a hand-held pencil, with very few upgrades over a great many years of use, is the same exciting, reliable, versatile and efficient artist's tool that it always was, long before its digital versions became available.

PRACTICAL EXERCISES

1. **Manipulate digital photographs**. Take digital photographs of some pieces of furniture in your home, and using bit-mapped graphics software such as Photoshop or Corel PHOTO-PAINT, lift the image of the furniture from the background and superimpose it onto a photograph of one of your hand-built set models, adjusting the size and colour as appropriate, and using a 'blend' tool to integrate it into the photograph and make the result look as realistic as possible. You may have to turn the furniture around before you photograph it so that the light hits it from approximately the same angle as in the photograph of the set model.

2. **Learn 3D digital modelling**. Download Google SketchUp from http://sketchup.google.com and work through the online tutorials.

3. **Make a 3D digital model of your home**. Measure the main pieces of furniture in your studio or workroom and, using whatever 3D modelling software you have available, construct accurate digital models of them. Next, make a digital model of your studio to contain the furniture you have made. You could then expand the model to include your entire house or flat. Then your street ...?

151

9 PRESENTATION

... when you got it, flaunt it.

Mel Brooks (1926–)

Working in the theatre, we are surrounded by people with expertise in presentation of one kind or another, from the actors to the Front of House Manager, and unfair though it may seem, the designer who can present his work proficiently stands a better chance of success than one of equal talent but lacking in presentation skills.

Presentation runs all through the designer's work: it is seen in the drawings distributed to technicians; the costume designs; the manner in which a scale model is displayed; the way concepts are explained to colleagues, and in a designer's portfolio of work to impress prospective employers. Good presentation can inspire confidence in a designer, and will tend to draw the best work from all those people whom designers depend upon to execute their ideas.

PORTFOLIOS AND INTERVIEWS

It is never too soon to start assembling a portfolio of your work, even if your only experience has been working on school plays or with a local amateur society. If you intend to apply for a theatre design course at a college or university, your success depends upon the examples of your work you show at an interview, so it is very important to keep copies of any design-related work you have done; also photographs of the shows you have worked on, and programmes and newspaper cuttings. These will later be replaced or supplemented in your portfolio by work you do at college, and later still, by your professional work. Designs that have actually been executed are always much more impressive than project work, so a good portfolio should include examples of your design work, accompanied by photographs showing the same work as it appeared on stage. When a designer becomes well-established, directors or theatre managers may be somewhat hesitant to ask to see a portfolio, so will probably be grateful if you offer some examples of your work. Limit your portfolio to a representative selection of your best work, instead of including pictures of every single piece of work you have ever done. Quality is always more impressive than quantity. Keep it neat and compact so that it is easy to carry around with you, and, preferably, small enough to lay out on a cluttered office desk. It can be very depressing for the interviewer when, having already interviewed many applicants, a candidate arrives with several

OPPOSITE: *Students from Theatre Design courses in the Department of Drama at the University of Alberta in Canada present their work to the public at the end-of-year Portfolio Show.*

153

large bags of work, which have to be unpacked on the floor and are clearly going to take a long time to work through. It is not a good idea to take models to interviews unless you are applying for a job as a model-maker, as they are unwieldy to transport, and usually impossible to display adequately in an interview situation. Take photographs of your models instead, and display them next to photographs of the completed set on stage. Resist the temptation to take your work on a CD or DVD to an interview. It may be convenient to transport, but there is no guarantee that the equipment to display it will be available, and if your interviewers are peering at the small screen of a laptop computer, you can easily find you that have lost their attention. Designs that can be handled and passed around are greatly preferable, but it is a very good idea to leave behind a disc containing all the work you have shown for their future reference, especially if the disc has an attractively designed sleeve, clearly displaying your name and contact details. The most convenient portfolios allow the work to be easily changed or rearranged.

An album with pages consisting of clear plastic pockets into which you can slip designs and photographs is a good choice. This means that you can prepare your portfolio in advance and be selective in the work you choose to show, giving greater emphasis to any work that is directly applicable to the job you are applying for. A director looking for a imaginative designer for a play by Strindberg may not be particularly interested in your beautifully produced technical drawings or designs for a pantomime cow, so take a selection of other kinds of work with you, but keep it somewhere handy so you can quickly produce it if the conversation moves in that direction. Clearly label every piece of work, and don't forget to place a label on the front of the portfolio with your name and contact details. When displaying production photographs, clearly state on the label what was your own particular contribution. Did you design the set? Costumes? Lighting? Allow the interviewer to look through your work at his or her own pace.

Avoid distracting chatter, but be ready to volunteer additional information about work in which any special interest is shown. Never be disparaging about your own work, even though you may be a naturally modest individual. You may sometimes feel slightly embarrassed to find the interviewer lingering over something you consider to be one of your least successful pieces of work, but avoid the temptation to point this out. If it is really bad it shouldn't be in your portfolio anyway. Tuck your business card and copies of your CV inside the portfolio so you can offer them to interviewers to keep if they wish. An interview is a marketing opportunity, and the product you are marketing is yourself and your talents as a designer.

PHOTOGRAPHS

Designers, especially set and costume designers, have the great advantage of being able to show pictures of their work. Actors, stage managers and directors cannot do this. They may show photographs of productions in which they have taken part, but they are actually showing the designer's work rather than their own. Look upon your digital camera as a valuable means of recording your work, but always use it with a professional consideration, and never take photographs at sensitive work sessions such as rehearsals or costume fittings without first asking permission from everyone involved, and don't forget to disable the flash. Most rehearsals demand sustained concentration from everyone involved, and a camera flash can be an infuriating intrusion.

If a photo-call with a professional photographer is arranged, you may like to ask him or her to take any special photographs you may require. At these sessions, the photographer usually concentrates closely on the actors, so may need to be prompted to take a full-stage photograph showing the entire set or full-length photographs of actors wearing your costumes.

Naturally, you will have to pay for prints, but don't forget to credit the photographer if they are reproduced in any printed matter or appear on your web site. You own the copyright of the design, but the photographer usually retains the copyright of the photographs.

PHOTOGRAPHING SET MODELS

Set models, even the most sturdily built ones, disintegrate over time, even if they manage to survive the rough and tumble they are usually subjected to in the rehearsal room or theatre workshops. In any case, if you are a reasonably successful designer, it will not be very long before the number of models outgrows the space you have available in which to store them, so get into the habit of photographing set models before they leave your studio to avoid tears when they lose those beautiful little details that took hours to make. Place the model at a convenient height so that, setting your camera on a tripod, you can photograph it from an audience member's point of view. Lighting can be provided by anglepoise or goose-necked desk lamps. Make a collection of off-cuts from coloured lighting gels to experiment with, especially if your model contains a cyclorama, for although most cycloramas are white or a pale neutral colour, the audience will usually see them only under tinted lighting, most frequently a pale bluish hue. This is best simulated by laying a piece of lighting gel over the back of the model, rather than placing it on the light source.

Diffusion or frosted gel can also be useful to eliminate unwanted shadows, and some scraps of Cinefoil or 'Black Wrap' (very thin, flexible, matt-black tin used for restricting light beams from luminaires) can sometimes be useful to confine the light from desk lamps to those small areas where it is needed.

PRESENTING YOUR WORK

Designers are usually required to present their work to various groups of people at different times. The first time will probably be at a production meeting, when a somewhat sceptical group of technicians and stage management will view it with wary eyes, and, totally ignoring your fine drafting, artistic costume renderings, and the finer details of your beautiful scale model, will be eager to point out any problems your work presents for their particular departments. It can be daunting, but you will also be asked to present your designs to the cast at the show's first rehearsal, and this time, you can expect one or two gratifying signs of admiration from the performers. However, be prepared to be cornered afterwards by individual actors who are concerned that the costume you have designed is not quite what they had in mind.

Designers are not generally happy as performers, so the prospect of having to stand up in front of a group of people to present and defend your work can be an intimidating experience. However, it forms a significant part of the job, and, like any other skill, it is one that improves with practice. Always prepare what you are going to say in advance: this does not mean learning a speech by heart, but simply mentally preparing the points you need to make. Building a scale model is a lengthy task, usually involving many repetitive activities, and these provide an excellent time to prepare your presentation in your head. Make notes if you have to, but never be tempted to read from them directly. Eye contact is important in any kind of communication, and you cannot maintain this while reading, so any notes should be confined to a simple list of headings just to jog your memory.

Starting a presentation is always the trickiest part, so if you are at all nervous, it is a good idea to give your confidence a boost by carefully preparing your very first sentence and learning it by heart, so you can avoid false starts and worrying hesitations. Do not start until you have everyone's complete attention. Make sure that everyone can hear you clearly by always aiming your words at the person who is sitting furthest away. If there is a large group, it might be difficult for everyone to see your designs, so after displaying them to the group, pass them around. If you have duplicated technical drawings, distribute them as soon as they are available, preferably before the production meeting, so that technicians can arrive already familiar with your designs. When presenting to the cast, remember that actors will be particularly anxious to see their costumes, so after you have shown each design to the group, pass it over to the actor playing the role for closer examination. A scale model can be difficult to show to a large group, so arrive early and set it up carefully in the

155

most convenient position, which should be at eye-level, with any light sources adjusted so that they light the model without shining into the viewers' eyes. Carry an extension cable with you, and bearing in mind that people are very likely to crowd around the model for a closer look after the presentation, always wrap light cables twice around a convenient table leg to prevent them bringing the model crashing to the floor if they get caught on someone's foot. Take care to aim your presentation specifically at the group of people you are addressing: the workshop technicians will not be at all interested in your idea that Macbeth is really all about the decadence underlying the politics of the Weimar Republic, but they will certainly be interested in the large tilted platform you have designed to represent it. Actors, on the other hand, may be quite interested in your concept, though it may be simply because they see themselves wearing lovely big leather boots. At the same time, the wardrobe supervisor will be wondering how the budget can be stretched to cover the cost of the boots, so confine your remarks

at production meetings to practicalities, and hold separate discussions about the details with department heads at a later stage. Always treat your designs with respect: if you handle the model with obvious care, and place the costume designs carefully on the table instead of casually throwing them down, you should find that your model suffers less damage in the workshops, and no one will scribble notes on your costume designs.

FITTING ROOM TECHNIQUE

The following notes are included in this section because the way the designer presents his or her work in the intimate confines of a fitting room can have a direct bearing upon the success or failure of his costume designs. A costume fitting is a time when all the participants are under some degree of stress. It is the first opportunity to judge the success, or otherwise, of a costume, and as designer, you will be anxious to see if your design has been interpreted as intended and get some impression of the total effect of the finished

A well-appointed fitting room in the Timms Centre for the Arts in Edmonton, Canada.

From time to time, you will encounter the tricky situation of having to fit a difficult or temperamental star actor into a costume that has had such a great deal of time and effort expended upon it that it becomes really essential that the actor approves it at the final fitting, as the wardrobe's resources have been entirely exhausted. Fortunately, most actors are not difficult and temperamental, so this is only a very infrequent occurrence. However, in the event, the following technique developed by the writer may be employed. Please note: this is a secret technique for use only in really desperate circumstances. It will lose its efficacy with over-use, so always use it with caution and do not circulate it unnecessarily. First, you must carefully prepare everyone working in the wardrobe department by explaining the simple role they are expected to play. When the actor arrives for the fitting, welcome him/her as usual, and if possible offer a drink (he may be exhausted by the rehearsals). Say how much you admire him for being able to cope with such a difficult role. Then accompany him into the fitting room, and get him to put on the costume, trying to keep his back to the mirror. (A mirror that can be folded away, such as the one in the photograph opposite, can be very useful here.) Before he has had time to examine the costume, say, 'I'm really sorry to ask this, but I wonder if you would mind letting the wardrobe staff see you wearing the costume they have been working on for so long?' The response can hardly be anything but assent. You then open the door and invite everyone in to have a look. If they play their parts well, they will stand in the doorway, gazing in obvious admiration and making remarks such as 'Oh, it's really, really beautiful!', 'Doesn't it look splendid?', 'All the hard work was worthwhile!' and so on. You then bundle them out, turn to the actor and say 'What do you think?' It's a really hard-hearted actor who can say he hates it after that.

costume. However, the costume supervisor needs to check if the costume fits well and estimate how much work remains to be done upon it, and at the same time, the performer is anxious to discover if the costume conforms to the interpretation of the role he or she has developed during rehearsals, and if the shoes are going to be comfortable. Under these rather tense circumstances, the designer needs to demonstrate tact, diplomacy and understanding, while, at the same time, making shrewd and instantaneous artistic judgements.

The finished costume will always look better on stage if the performer is happy wearing it, so it is worthwhile making an effort to retain the performer's trust. To do this, the designer should show some elementary courtesies: be ready to greet the actor when he arrives for the fitting; show the design again with the costume he is to try on, explaining what work is still to be done. Sometimes a calico mock-up of the costume has to be fitted before cutting into the actual fabric, so, if this is the case, make quite sure that the performer understands that this will bear little resemblance to the finished costume, and you are asking for his co-operation in a purely technical process. The fitting room should be clean and tidy, with large mirrors, good lighting, and at least one chair for performers to sit on when trying on footwear.

When the performer has been fitted into the costume, ask him to try sitting, raising his arms, and, if he is required to perform any unusual actions such as jumping, fighting, or falling on the floor, encourage him to try them while wearing the costume. Most performers will appreciate a little time alone in the fitting room to get the feel of their costume in private, and you can tactfully arrange this by leaving the room for a minute or two to search for accessories such as a belt or tie. Listen carefully to any comments or suggestions, and attempt to incorporate them if they are reasonable and practical.

YOUR WEB SITE

As a professional designer you will need a business web site, containing contact details, your CV, and an online portfolio of your work. There are a great many web hosting companies offering a variety of packages for renting web space and setting up domain names, usually with several related email addresses and various other facilities (you will find them in your Yellow Pages), but beware of paying for more space than you will actually need. Many packages are aimed at business or corporate institutions requiring a large number of pages and linked sub-sites, which need far more space than you will ever use, so consider buying the smallest package on offer to begin with and extend it by renting additional space if or when you need it.

The author has used the London-based web hosting company, Corpex (http://www.corpex.com) for many years, and has found them to be helpful and efficient. When you rent some space from a web hosting company, your address (or URL) will, by default, contain the name of the company, such as www.webhost.com/~myname/; however, you will create a far better impression on prospective employers if you pay a small charge to register your own domain name, and ask your web hosting company to create a 'virtual domain' for you on their server, so that your URL becomes something like: www.myname.com. Choose a name logically based upon your own professional name, and avoid anything cute or jokey that may raise a wan smile but will do little to suggest a professional approach to your work. You cannot use spaces or most punctuation marks in web site addresses, and it is also a good idea to avoid under-scorings in domain names or email addresses, such as 'my_name.com', as these are frequently displayed on-screen with automatic underlining that will hide the under-scores and inevitably cause confusion. Make sure your web site is easy to navigate, even for people with only very basic Internet skills. It should be possible for a visitor to access any information they are looking for with no more than three clicks of the mouse, and every page should contain a clearly displayed direct link back to the Home page. Your site is there primarily to give information about you and your abilities as a theatre designer, so do not be tempted to decorate it with distracting animations or showy effects that have no relevance to your work. As your site is intended to present you as a competent and professional designer, it is also advisable to avoid pictures of your pet or your baby, no matter how cute they may be – and never include music. When your site has been designed and thoroughly checked on your own computer, you will be ready to upload it to the server where you have rented your web space and make it available to the World Wide Web. To do this you will need to use a special FTP (File Transfer Protocol) programme specifically designed for exchanging and manipulating files over the Internet. One of the most popular and user-friendly of these is Cute FTP from Globalscape, which is available in several versions, including a version for Macs, at a reasonable cost, with a thirty-day free trial, from their web site at http://www.cuteftp.com.

DESIGNING YOUR OWN WEB SITE

You can design your own site with a programme such as Adobe's Dreamweaver, available for both the Windows and Mac operating systems, but it is a great advantage to learn the web site programming language, originally HTML (HyperText Mark-up Language), but now generally supplanted by XHTML (Extensible HyperText Mark-up Language). It is not difficult to learn, and not only enables you to create web pages from scratch, without the need for any special software other than a basic word processor, but also makes regular updating quick and easy. This is important, as 'dead' links and out-of-date information can create a really bad impression.

If you right-click anywhere on a web site, but avoiding pictures, and select 'View Source' from the menu that pops up you will usually see a lot of pretty coloured text similar to that in the illustration opposite, which is a small section of code taken from the writer's own web site. The illustration opposite shows what this code produces. You cannot simply create a page layout for a web site using, say, Microsoft Word, and upload it directly to the server, in spite of the fact that, along with some other word-processors, it offers the option to save files to HTML format. In practice, this hardly ever works as intended, and even when it does, it creates huge amounts of inefficient code in the attempt. You are strongly

```
23      <img src="3dpics/3dmod1.jpg" valign="top" align="left" hspace="5" width="350"
        height="238" title="Set model &#39;printed&#39; by 3D printer">
24      <img src="3dpics/3dmod6.jpg" valign="top" align="right" hspace="5" width="350"
        height="238" title="Set model &#39;printed&#39; by 3D printer">
25
26  <br clear="all">
27  <br>
28      <p align="justify">
29        Many theatre designers now use CAD programmes to produce their plans and
        working drawings, and <i>AutoCAD</i> is generally considered to be the industry
        standard software. Those of us who have explored a little beyond the basics
        will have discovered the advantages of 3D modelling&#58;
30        A digital model can be constructed on&#45;screen, from which hard copies of
        plans, elevations, sections, isometric or perspective views can be printed out
        at any scale, from the same model, &#45; almost literally &#39;at the touch of
        a button&#39;.
31        <br><br>
32        Recent technological advances now permit us to take a spectacular step
        further&#58; Computing and Network Services here at the University of Alberta
        in Canada has a <i>Zcorp Z400</i> 3D printer which will convert a digital model
        into a remarkably detailed tangible object model. <i>&#40;Photographs
        above&#41;</i>
33      </p>
```

A small section of source code.

Many theatre designers now use CAD programmes to produce their plans and working drawings, and *AutoCAD* is generally considered to be the industry standard software. Those of us who have explored a little beyond the basics will have discovered the advantages of 3D modelling: A digital model can be constructed on-screen, from which hard copies of plans, elevations, sections, isometric or perspective views can be printed out at any scale, from the same model, - almost literally 'at the touch of a button'.

Recent technological advances now permit us to take a spectacular step further: Computing and Network Services here at the University of Alberta in Canada has a *Zcorp Z400* 3D printer which will convert a digital model into a remarkably detailed tangible object model. *(Photographs above)*

Part of a web page produced by the code in the previous illustration.

advised to ignore it. In fact, you should not use high-level word processors at all when creating source code, as these save much formatting information along with the text; this merely confuses the HTML, which uses entirely different formatting techniques. It is far more convenient to use a really basic word processor such as Microsoft's Notepad.

You can use Mac's TextEdit, but you must save the files in plain-text format to remove any built-in formatting. Best of all, are the text-editors specially created for writing source code, such as Notepad++, which you can download for free from http://notepad-plus.sourceforge.net. Basic HTML code is designed to contain text and pictures to be displayed as web pages, along with instructions describing how they are to be displayed by web-browsers, and create active 'links', or those places where users need to point and click to change the page in some way or move to another page. To do this, sections of text or pictures are commonly enclosed in 'tags', which are the instructions to be carried out by the browser. These tags are typically set between angle-brackets and arranged in pairs, consisting of an 'opening' tag such as <i> and a 'closing' tag such as </i>, which in this case, instruct the browser to display the words between the tags in italics. (See line 29 in the source code on page 159.) You may feel slightly confused by the frequently recurring term, CSS (Cascading Style Sheets), whenever web site programming is discussed. This is a powerful technique used in conjunction with XHTML that, among other things, helps the designer to format pages in a way that makes them compatible with almost any type of browser, and makes it easy to make changes to the appearance of text throughout a site consisting of many pages by adjusting a single piece of source code that is common to them all, instead of having to change each page individually. Eventually, you might like to try a scripting language, such as JavaScript, originally developed by Netscape and now included as standard with most browsers. JavaScript offers many neat effects such as animated 'buttons' and pictures that change when the mouse-pointer passes over them, but you will need to know (X)HTML to use this, so leave it until you have acquired some experience in the basics. Note that JavaScript is not at all the same as Java, which is an expert's programming language that requires a good deal of technical skill to use. Take care not to get them confused. The techniques involved in programming web sites are not difficult to acquire, though far too involved to attempt to teach here, but if these few paragraphs have given

you an urge to learn to write your own code in HTML or its much more versatile and up-to-date version, XHTML, you should buy one of the books recommended in the Bibliography at the end of this book. Those by Elizabeth Castro and Andy Harris both include excellent, easy to understand, tutorials, including chapters on JavaScript, and a CD containing the examples described in the text along with some useful free software.

GETTING YOUR SITE LISTED BY THE SEARCH ENGINES

At the top of the source code for every web page you will see a rather puzzling section contained between the tags <head> and </head>. This is important information about the page that is not intended to be displayed on-screen. Some lines of this code are to help the site to be discovered by search engines such as Yahoo and Google. Search engines have little robot programmes called 'spiders' that continually roam about the World Wide Web looking for unlisted sites. When they find one, they automatically add it to the search engine's lists, attempting to estimate the appropriate place to include it and how to classify it. You can help by including some information about your site for special consideration by the search engines in the form of 'meta tags'. In the 'head' sections of the writer's web pages you will find the following lines (as with all HTML source code, line breaks are irrelevant):

```
<meta name='description'
content='Personal site of UK theatre
designer Colin Winslow, containing a
portfolio of his designs for stage
settings and costumes' /> <meta
name='keywords' content='winslow,
theatre, theater, theatrical, design,
designer, designs, setting, settings,
scene, scenery, scenic, stage, staging,
scenography, scenografie, costume,
costumes, musical, opera, ballet, play,
show, decor, decorateur, ontwerp,
toneel, decorontwerper, crowood, model,
making' />
```

In the first line, 'description' contains a short descriptive sentence that can be used by search engines when listing the site. Without this, they will usually display the first line of text on the page instead, which may not be quite so appropriate. It is, however, a good idea to make sure that the first line of text on your Home page is something appropriately descriptive in case a search engine uses this technique. In the next line, 'keywords' allows you to list up to 250 words that are likely to be used by anyone searching for a site such as yours. Note that words that are most likely to be used such as 'theatre' and 'design', are included in several languages, including the American spelling of 'theater'. If you have set up a temporary site for a specific show as described on page 150 you may prefer it not to be listed by the search engines. In this case, include the line:

```
<meta name='robots' content='noindex,
no follow' />
```

in the 'head' section. This will make the spiders ignore the page and send them scurrying off to some other part of the web.

EXHIBITING YOUR WORK

Designers are frequently presented with the opportunity to show their work in exhibitions of one kind or another. If you are a student, this may be a Graduation Show, or as a professional designer, it may be at an event such as the Prague Quadrennial (PQ) international exhibition of performance design, or it could be just a chance to show a set model and some costume designs in the foyer of the theatre where a production you have designed is playing. Whatever it is, you should look upon it as a valuable marketing opportunity, so make sure your work is presented as attractively as possible. Models always look best viewed from eye-level and well lit, even if only from a carefully positioned desk-lamp. Some visitors will be unable to resist prodding your models with a finger, or even attempting to steal small items, so make sure all furniture and moveable parts are firmly fixed in place. All your work should be clearly labelled with

the name of the show, and above all, make sure your own name is boldly displayed in some very obvious position. Leave a stack of printed flyers or business cards for visitors to pick up and take away with them. You should never be hesitant to market your talent, for it will be wasted if no one gets to know about it. The modest, retiring person might, in fact, be the better designer, but often, unfair though it seems, it is the one who presents himself and his work in an outgoing and professional manner who usually gets the best jobs.

If directors or some other prospective employers show an interest in your work, ask for their contact details, and send them a postcard or an email thanking them for their interest, and asking if they would like to arrange a meeting to look at more of your work. Keep a list of all the contacts you make so that at Christmas or New Year you can send each of them, and anyone you have worked for during the previous year, a greetings card with one of your most attractive designs printed on it, together with a reminder of your name, telephone number, email and web site address. It may be a little expensive, but it only needs to produce one job to pay off, and anyway, it's tax-deductible!

PRACTICAL EXERCISES

1. **Create a portfolio.** It is a temptation to leave this until you need it for an interview, but this can easily result in one that looks hastily assembled and does not show your work at its best. If you design more than one element, such as set and costumes, or set and lighting, buy a folder for each of them. You might also like to keep a portfolio showing examples of any special skills you may have, such as model-making, scene-painting or CAD, if you intend to look for work in these areas or as an assistant designer.

2. **Experiment with HTML.** Using a basic word processor such as Notepad or TextEdit, carefully type the following code exactly as it appears here. The size and style of font is irrelevant, but you must remember to use the American spelling of 'color' and 'center':

```
<html> <head>  <title>My web
page</title> </head>  <body
bgcolor='olive'>  <font color='white'>
<h1 align='center'>MY WEB PAGE</h1>
</font>  <br>  <font color='black'
size='4'>  <p align='center'>  <img
src='c/pictures/set picture.jpg'
alt='Picture of stage set'>  <br>  <b>Put
your own text here.</b>  <br><br>  <i>You
can put more text here if you wish.</i>
</p> </font>  </body> </html>
```

Save it as a plain-text HTM file. That is, go to 'Save As ...', give it a name such as 'My First Web Page', but instead of accepting the default three-letter file extension offered by the software, type in .htm instead, then save the file to your hard drive. Find the file's icon on your screen and click on it. Your computer should then open it as a web page that looks like the illustration below. As you are running it from your hard drive, you don't have to be online to see it. Next, load the code again into Notepad or TextEdit by right-clicking on its icon and selecting it from the 'Open with ...' option in the pop-up menu. You can now experiment with substituting your own text and changing the colours of background and fonts. (Acceptable colour-names are aqua, black, blue, fuchsia, gray, green, lime, maroon, navy, olive, purple, red, silver, teal, white and yellow.) You can also add a picture by typing its name and the path to it on your own computer in place of 'c/pictures/set picture.jpg'. Don't forget the inverted commas and the file extension, and don't make the picture too big: the one displayed in the example below is 600 × 388 pixels. Save it again as an .htm file, and display the web page by left-clicking on its icon. Note that what you have just written is a small piece of very basic HTML, and is not ready to be uploaded to the World Wide Web. You need to know much more about XHTML and CSS before you can do this.

3. **Join the Society of British Theatre Designers** to show your CV and pictures of your work on its web site at http://www.theatredesign.org.uk and receive its quarterly magazine, *The Blue Pages.*

Sample web page displayed as indicated by the basic HTML code in the text above.

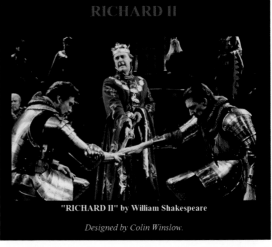

Sample web page with picture and text added, and the colours of fonts and background adjusted.

APPENDIX

CONSTRUCTING A PERSPECTIVE SET RENDERING BASED UPON A STAGE PLAN

A perspective rendering can be constructed technically using a stage plan, and will often be found useful in giving a reasonably accurate impression of a set on stage. Follow these steps:

1. Draw the proscenium opening to scale and mark the vertical centre-line.
2. Mark off intervals of 50cm (or 1ft if working in imperial measurements) at the same scale along the base line and up one side of the proscenium opening.
3. Assume the viewer to be standing at the centre of the auditorium and, estimating the viewer's eye-level, mark the horizon line at eye-level right across the page. If the viewer is standing centrally, the vanishing point will fall at the intersection of the horizon line with the vertical centre-line. Draw perspective lines through the marks along the base line of the proscenium to the vanishing point.
4. Mark a point on the horizon line equivalent to the distance from the viewer to the proscenium, measuring outwards from the vanishing point to left or right along the horizon line (DP).
5. Extend a line from DP to the bottom corner of the proscenium on the opposite side.
6. Draw horizontal lines through the points where the diagonal intersects the perspective lines to construct a grid of 50cm (or 1ft) squares in perspective.
7. The set may now be plotted on this perspective grid from a similar (non-perspective) grid drawn on the stage plan.
8. Take all vertical measurements from the proscenium and extend lines back towards the vanishing point to estimate heights of objects in perspective.

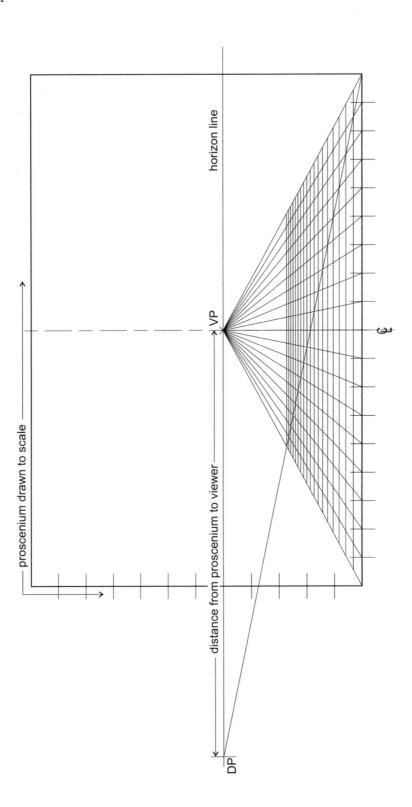

Perspective floor grid constructed on elevation of proscenium, drawn to scale.

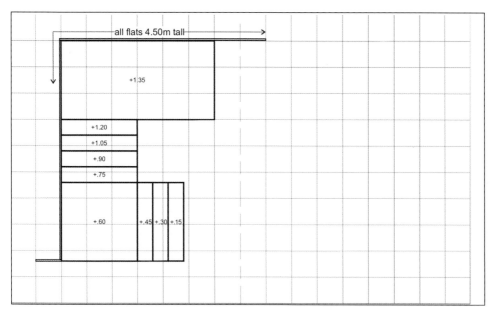

all flats 4.50m tall

+1.35

+1.20
+1.05
+.90
+.75
+.60   +.45 +.30 +.15

Plan of structure with superimposed grid of 50cm squares drawn to scale.

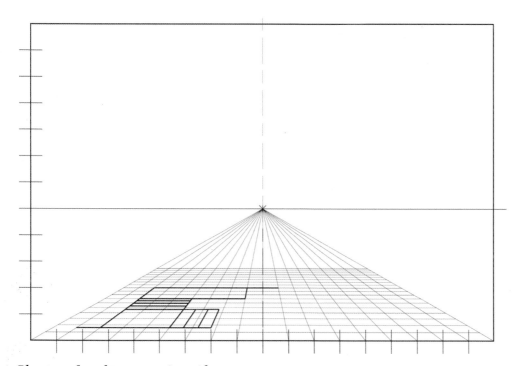

Plan transferred to perspective grid.

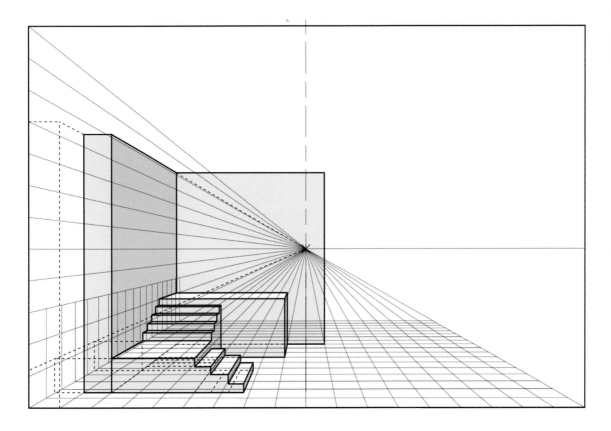

Structure rendered in perspective before removal of construction lines.

BIBLIOGRAPHY

STAGE DESIGN

Bay, H., *Stage Design* (Pitman Publishing, 1974)

Blumenthal, E., Julie Taymor *Playing with Fire* (Harry N. Abrams Inc., 1999)

Burian, J., *The Scenography of Josef Svoboda* (Wesleyan University Press, 1971)

Goodwin, J., *British Theatre Design, The Modern Age* (George Weidenfeld and Nicolson Ltd., 1989)

Mielziner J., *Designing for the Theatre: A Memoir and a Portfolio* (Bramhall House, 1965)

Pecktal, L., *Designing and Painting for the Theatre* (Holt, Rinehart and Winston Inc., 1975)

Reid, F., *Designing for the Theatre* (A & C Black Ltd., 1996)

Rosenfeld, S., *A Short History of Scene Design in Great Britain* (Basil Blackwell, 1973)

Winslow, C., *The Handbook of Set Design* (The Crowood Press, 2006)

RESEARCH

Amery, C., *Period Houses and their Details* (The Architectural Press, 1974)

Calloway, S., *The Elements of Style: An Encyclopedia of Domestic Architectural Detail* (Firefly Books Ltd., 2005)

Campbell, C., *Vitruvius Britannicus* (Dover Publications Inc., 2007)

Ching, F.D.K., *A Visual Dictionary of Architecture* (John Wiley & Sons, Inc., 1995)

Gloag, J., *The Crystal Palace Exhibition*, Illustrated Catalogue, London (1851) (Dover Publications Inc., 1970)

Meyer, F.S., *Handbook of Ornament* (Dover Publications Inc., 1957)

Speltz, A., *The Styles of Ornament* (Dover Publications Inc., 1959)

DRAWING AND SKETCHING

Barber, B., *The Fundamentals of Drawing* (Arcturus Publishing Ltd., 2007)

Hale, R.B., *Anatomy Lessons from the Great Masters* (Watson-Guptill Publications, 2000)

Hale, R.B., *Drawing Lessons from the Great Masters* (Watson-Guptill Publications, 1989)

Petroski, H., *The Pencil* (Alfred A. Knopf, 1992)

Raynes, J., *Complete Anatomy and Figure Drawing* (Batsford, 2007)

COLOUR

Finlay, V., *Colour* (Hodder and Stoughton, 2002)

Garfield, S., *Mauve* (Faber and Faber Ltd., 2000)

Jennings, S., *Artist's Colour Manual* (Harper Collins, 2003)

Lüscher, M., *The Lüscher Colour Test* (Jonathan Cape Ltd., 1970)

Sloane, P., *Colour: Basic Principles and New Directions* (Studio Vista, 1967)

DRAFTING AND TECHNICAL DRAWING

Ching, F.D.K., *Design Drawing* (John Wiley & Sons Inc., 1998)

Ching, F.D.K., *Architectural Graphics* (Van Nostrand Reinhold Company, 1975)

Rose, R., *Drafting Scenery for Theater, Film and Television* (Betterway Books, 1990)

MODEL-MAKING

Mills, C.B., *Designing with Models, A Studio Guide to Making and Using Architectural Design Models*

(John Wiley & Sons Inc., 2005)

Mulvany, K. and Rogers S., *Magnificent Miniatures: Inspiration and Technique for Grand Houses on a Small Scale* (Batsford 2008)

Payne, D.R., *Theory and Craft of the Scenographic Model* (Southern Illinois University Press, 1976)

Robinson, J.M., *Queen Mary's Dolls' House, Official Guidebook* (Royal Collection Enterprises, Ltd., 2006)

Winslow, C., *The Handbook of Model-making for Set Designers* (The Crowood Press, 2008)

TEXTURES AND PATTERNS

Hoskins, L., *The Papered Wall* (Harry N. Abrams Inc., 1994)

Juracek, J.A., *Surfaces: Visual Research for Artists, Architects and Designers* (W.W. Norton & Co. Ltd., 1996)

Juracek, J.A., *Soft Surfaces: Visual Research for Artists, Architects and Designers* (W.W. Norton & Co. Ltd., 2000)

Juracek, J.A., *Architectural Surfaces: Details for Artists, Architects and Designers* (W.W. Norton & Co. Ltd., 2005)

PERSPECTIVE

Kemp, M., *The Science of Art: Optical Themes in Western Art from Brunelleschi to Seurat* (Yale University Press, 1990)

Raynes, J., *The Complete Guide to Perspective* (Collins and Brown, 2005)

COSTUME DESIGN

Blum, S., *Victorian Fashions and Costumes from Harper's Bazar: 1867–1898* (Dover Publications Inc., 1974)

Bradfield, N., *Historical Costumes of England, 1066–1968* (Eric Dobby Publishing Ltd., 1995)

Braun and Schneider, *Historic Costume in Pictures* (Dover Publications Inc., 1975)

Kybalova, L., *The Pictorial Encyclopedia of Fashion* (The Hamlyn Publishing Group Ltd., 1972)

Tortora, P. and Eubank, K., *Survey of Historic Costume* (Fairchild Publications Inc., 2005)

DIGITAL TECHNIQUES

Ambrosius, L., *AutoCAD 2008 3D Modelling Workbook for Dummies* (Wiley Publishing Inc., 2007)

Brito, A., *Blender 3D: Architecture, Buildings, and Scenery* (Packt Publishing, 2008)

Carver, G. and White, C., *Computer Visualization for the Theatre: 3D Modelling for Designers* (Focal Press 2003)

Chopra, A., *Google SketchUp 7 for Dummies* (Wiley Publishing Inc., 2009)

McFarland, J. and Simon, J., *Master Visually 3ds Max 8* (Wiley Publishing Inc., 2006)

Ripley, D., *AutoCAD – A Handbook for Theatre Users* (Entertainment Technology Press Ltd., 2004)

Tyler, D., *Practical Poser 7* (Charles River Media, 2007)

van Gumster, J., *Blender for Dummies* (Wiley Publishing Inc., 2009)

WEB SITE DESIGN

Castro, E., *HTML, XHTML and CSS, Sixth Edition: Visual Quickstart Guide* (Peachpit Press, 2007)

Castro, E. and Negrino, T., *JavaScript for the World Wide Web: Visual Quickstart Guide* (Peachpit Press, 2006)

Flanders, V. and Willis, M., *Web Pages That Suck: Learn Good Design by Looking at Bad Design* (Sybex, 1998)

Harris, A. *HTML, XHTML, and CSS All-in-One Desktop Reference for Dummies* (Wiley Publishing Inc., 2008)

McClelland, D., Eismann, K. and Stone, T., *Web Design Studio Secrets, 2nd Edition* (IDG Books Worldwide Inc., 2000)

USEFUL WEB SITES

http://www.abtt.org.uk
The Association of British Theatre Technicians (ABTT). A professional organization covering all fields of theatre technology – including health and safety issues. Stacks of useful stuff, and a good 'Green Room' discussion forum.

http://get.adobe.com/reader
Download the free Adobe Reader software for reading PDF documents here.

http://www.ald.org.uk
The Association of Lighting Designers (ALD). The professional body representing lighting designers in all fields in the UK and the rest of the world.

http://www.anellodavide.com
Anello and Davide. London firm providing all types of footwear for the stage, including ballet shoes. Their catalogue of period footwear (available online) is particularly useful as a quick reference resource.

http://www.angels.uk.com
Angels the Costumiers. London-based firm with the largest collection of costumes and accessories anywhere in the world. Costume hire for productions of any size.

http://www.artquest.org.uk/artlaw.htm
Artlaw is an excellent online resource offering free legal advice to artists and craftspeople. The site contains the thirty most frequently asked questions with expert legal answers.

http://www.bltrimmings.com
Barnett Lawson Trimmings Ltd. in central London, stocks a very wide range of braids, buttons, feathers, fringes, etc. An illustrated catalogue with an online sampling service available.

http://www.borovickfabricsltd.co.uk
Borovick Fabrics Ltd., a long-established family firm in central London, specializing in supplying fabrics for the entertainment industries. A free sampling service is available.

http://wwww.cad4theatre.org.uk
Run by David Ripley, this site provides online AutoCAD training for the theatre and entertainment industries. The site includes the freely downloadable ABTT standards for CAD. http://www.corpex.com Corpex Ltd., UK firm offering Web Hosting and Domain Name services.

http://www.crowood.com
The Crowood Press, publishers of this book and many others on technical theatre subjects.

http://www.cuteftp.com
Home of Cute FTP software by Gobalscape. Inexpensive software for uploading files to web sites etc. Versions for PC and Mac operating systems are available with thirty days' free trial.

http://www.equity.org.uk
Equity, the trade union representing professional performers and other creative workers in the entertainment industries. The SBTD is affiliated to Equity, and all theatre designers are strongly recommended to join.

http://www.fieldtemplate.com
Field-Templates in New York, suppliers of imperial scale lighting templates.

http://www.siue.edu/COSTUMES/history.html
The History of Costume, the celebrated nineteenth-century costume reference book by Braun and Schneider online.

http://www.modelshop.co.uk
The 4D Model Shop under the arches in Leman Street, London, stocking practically everything you could possibly need for making set models. Includes a detailed online catalogue.

http://notepad-plus.sourceforge.net
Download the free source code editor Notepad++ here.

http://www.paperchase.co.uk
> Nationwide chain of stores specializing in all kinds of paper and art materials.

http://www.plastruct.com
> Plastruct Inc., international supplier of plastic scale model parts based in the USA. An online catalogue is available.

http://www.rosco.com
> Rosco International, suppliers of products such as stage lighting equipment, including gels and gobos, smoke and fog machines, scene paints, and much more.

http://www.techsoft.co.uk
> Based in Denbighshire, TechSoft supply CAD and CAD/CAM software and hardware, including 3D printers and laser cutters.

http://www.theatredesign.org.uk
> Official site of The Society of British Theatre Designers (SBTD) including details of membership, forthcoming events, and a list of members with their contact details, many showing pictures of their work.

http://www.thestage.co.uk
> *The Stage*, the long-established weekly newspaper of the theatrical profession.

http://www.ualberta.ca/CNS/3DPRINTER
> Home of the Spectrum Z510 colour 3D printer at the University of Alberta.

http://www.uktw.co.uk
> UK Theatre Web, with useful information about what's happening on the British theatre scene.

http://www.vl-theatre.com
> The Theatre and Drama section of the World Wide Web's Virtual Library, containing pointers to a broad range of theatrical resources across the world.

http://www.wga.hu
> The Web Gallery of Art, containing thousands of digital reproductions of European paintings and sculptures from 1150 to 1800, many with commentaries and biographies, also some 'guided tours'.

http://www.whitelight.ltd.uk
> White Light Ltd. UK firm supplying everything electrical for the theatrical profession.

http://www.winslow.uk.com
> The author's personal web site.

http://www.zcorp.com
> Suppliers of 3D printers, scanners and software.

LIST OF ILLUSTRATIONS

LIST OF ILLUSTRATIONS

INDEX

INDEX